THE COURAGE
TO BE DIFFERENT

LESSONS IN
OVERCOMING ADVERSITY

SECOND EXPANDED EDITION

I.VICENTE

VC

PUBLISHING

ISBN: 978-0-9916552-5-0

Book edited by Reba Hilbert

Cover design by Stephane Coic, Paris and Mexico City

Book layout by www.ebooklaunch.com

Photos in the book from author's collection

Front photography from Shutterstock

Back photo of author by Michelle Mueth

ALSO BY I.VICENTE

The Courage to be Different
(First Edition)

Divergent Lives

For all the young people, and grown-ups too,
who struggle to cope with a disadvantaged past
and want to chart a new path in their lives.

"I learned that courage was not the absence of fear, but the triumph over it. The brave man is not he who does not feel afraid, but he who conquers that fear."

- Nelson Mandela

Preface to the Second Edition

As I listened to readers of *The Courage to Be Different*, I was delighted to hear that they wanted to know more about certain events that the book exposes. Some expressed a desire to know more about my successes as an adult, and some wanted to know more about my experiences as a single father. Friends who know that I was a single parent and thought that the experience in itself must have taken a great deal of courage wanted to read more about that part of my life. My brother, Wil, whom I love very much, thought that some of the events described could use more details. Having lived through many of the stories, he remembered additional details that I had left out, simply because they did not permeate my recollection. I was pleased that he and my sister, Susan, were supportive of my divulging the dysfunction that was our childhood and adolescence.

There was no question in my mind that a second edition was in order. For one, it allows me to expand on relationships with friends as I struggled with the demons I unwillingly collected as a child. A big part of my upbringing were the lessons I learned upon seeing my mother's spiritualistic practices. I relayed in the book the Santeria practices at my friend Jose's house, but did not include that Mom was a Puerto Rican spiritualist, more commonly referred to today as a medium. Readers of the second edition will have a more complete view into the world I grew up in.

A number of readers have told me that they passed the book around to younger teenage members of their families.

They found my story to be sad, but inspirational for their own parenting. The revisions to the book will hopefully be even more inspiring to young people who may be struggling with their own family life and with the decision to muster up the courage to chart their own path. I will be immensely delighted if the book can help these struggling young people through their own journey from a life of poverty and pain to one of prosperity and love. And I mean that in both the physical and the spiritual sense.

My inspiration for writing this book in the first place was the realization that regardless of the success I have been fortunate to enjoy through hard work and obstinate, but focused, perseverance, the demons of my young life would not leave me. This is my way of facing them up close and telling them, "Get out!" I am not a believer in psychotherapy, and therefore have never been inclined to sit down with a "professional" and tell and retell my life story to someone who would be paid to listen, but could not offer real solutions. They may be happy to listen to me, with a stopwatch by their side to make sure I did not exceed my allotted time. They might ask, "…and how do you feel telling me that?"

It may work for some people, but not for me.

It was my destiny to release the demons of my childhood and adolescence through the writing of this book. As the pages filled with the vividness of my memories and the history that is my life, I could sense internal pressure releasing from my head, through my chest, my gut, and finally exiting through my fingertips. It has been an amazingly rewarding process.

So, it is my sincere hope that the second edition, with its more elaborate detail, will inspire many young people to find their way to a happy life, and not feel guilt, or reservation, in finding the courage to be different.

Prologue

The idea for *The Courage to Be Different* came to me as I lay in the critical care unit of Somerset Medical Center (now Robert Wood Johnson) in New Jersey after I experienced a heart attack in September 2012. I realized that I had spent far too many years feeling sorry for myself for having been raised in a destructive manner. In many ways, I have been blessed with success, a beautiful family, and a small circle of caring friends. Yet, I have never shared with any of them the history that is my life. If I had died when I suffered that heart attack, no one would know the details of my background. No one would know why and how I grew up to be the person that I was. Most importantly, no benefit would be reaped by other young people who might be facing the same struggles and challenges that I faced as a child and young adult.

My condition awakened in me a need to share with anyone who might be interested in how I grew up and my journey through the annals of poverty, family strife, doubt, insecurity, and ultimately success.

There are so many stories of my childhood that have swirled in my mind for all these years—some good, and many bad. Sharing these stories with readers affords me the opportunity to understand why they might have happened. Friends tell me that my parents did the best they could, that perhaps they raised my four siblings and me the way their parents raised them.

It is true that for most people the world they grew up in is not that different from what they create for their own children. The complexity is that the times and the environment by which we are surrounded do change. That adds a level of influence that may make a parent's job more difficult, unless they recognize that times are different and therefore they cannot expect their children to grow up as they did.

As one example, play time has changed quite dramatically from the days when I was a kid in the sixties and seventies. Back then if our parents wanted us out of the way, they might say, "Go outside and play." Today, they might say, "Go get on the iPad and play." It is quite a different world.

What my friends perhaps cannot comprehend is that this rationalization is not sufficient for me to be able to accept that it is what it is and move on. I need something more profound than that in order to come to terms with my own history. A big part of coming to terms with my past is to discover how to forgive my parents. That is important as they live the twilight of their lives. Not only do I want to live in peace with my own life, and my own history, but I want them to live their final years peacefully within as well.

My dad is now eighty-four and my mom is seventy-nine. They live in a one-bedroom apartment in Astoria, New York. They live as simply as they have always lived, comforted daily by their Chihuahua and Dad's fish tank, strategically placed adjacent to the television set. He can watch the ballgame while keeping an eye on his assortment of goldfish as he rocks back and forth in his signature rocking chair—perhaps not so ironically as his mom and dad rocked in theirs back in Mayaguez, Puerto Rico. Mom spends most of her time in the lobby's prayer room, holding court with other elderly neighbors as she leads them in daily prayers.

Their eyes light up with the occasional visit from one of their kids. On extra special occasions, perhaps Thanksgiving or Christmas, more than one of us stops by at the same time. Mom and Dad love those occasions. It gives them a warm sense of having a family reunion.

It is for their sake, as well as mine, and hopefully my brothers and sisters, that I write this book. Since I have never believed in psychological counseling, this is my best attempt at therapy. I have never thought that telling my life's story to a stranger and expecting answers to my many questions was a good idea. No one knows me better than I know myself, or so I have always thought.

Besides, while the questions "Why did they do that?" or "How could they do that?" might have been important at the time a certain act was perpetrated, it no longer seems important to answer those questions.

Had those questions been asked at the appropriate time, they would have had to have been asked by the right person, an adult, in the interest of intervention; that might have changed the history of my life. But that was not my destiny. My destiny was to live through all of the experiences I will share in this book. Those experiences might have been essential to ignite the flame of determination, perseverance, and hunger that made me who I am today.

I was not a child raised with love, caring, self-confidence, integrity, respect, patience, understanding, unselfishness, and trust—all of those attributes that are supposed to serve as a solid foundation in a child's life. Instead, I remember a childhood filled with hate, violence, deceit, fear, disrespect, cheating, negative criticism, selfishness, and impatience.

It was a confusing life. I loved my mom and dad, as children do, but could not understand why they did things to hurt me or my siblings. There were good times, of course, but as human nature will dictate, pain is much more easily remembered for its dramatic and emotional impact. Not to mention its scars. Loving care by parents is appreciated, but it is also expected. As children, even as adults, we want more of that. We learn at an early age to reciprocate with the same emotions and behavior with which we are bestowed and therefore taught.

When we as children are treated by our parents in a hurtful, violent manner, physically and emotionally, that is what we learn and how we reciprocate. That is how we learn to treat others in school, the playground, and even at home among siblings. That is the reality and the epidemic facing inner-city neighborhoods all over America, including ours in the South Bronx and East Elmhurst, Queens.

It has taken me well into my forties and even fifties to try to undo the damage from years of an abusive upbringing. All of my adult life I have worked to become a better person. That has sometimes been a struggle. My mission through the years has been to become a better father, husband, friend, brother, colleague, and boss. In order to accomplish my mission, I have had to confront my demons repeatedly. I think that I have managed to get rid of some. But others still linger. Demons have a proclivity to be obstinate.

As long as my demons are inside of me, they will win some of the battles we wage against each other. I have had to be brutally honest with myself about that. These demons have a very resilient makeup. They are constructed of genetics, which are by nature impossible to eliminate, and by the shape my parents molded me into when I was a child and adolescent.

It is entirely possible, I suppose, for someone to be satisfied with being what they were raised to be. They can somehow accept that this is who they are, and are content to live their life that way. I saw that in some of my siblings who felt they could not move away from the old neighborhood and didn't feel they were good enough or smart enough to do better for themselves.

It is well documented and manifested each and every day that more often than not, children will grow up to follow in their parents' footsteps. They will "inherit," through daily interaction that serves to mold them, the qualities of their parents. This has been human nature since the beginning of time. Even the Gospels are filled with examples of sons following in their fathers' footsteps as early as the first century. Remember that Jesus was a carpenter like his father, Joseph, even though he had a much different calling ultimately.

Mom and Dad quit school in the eighth grade. My older brother, Nelson, was the first of the five of us to get to high school, but he dropped out of Newtown H.S. in the ninth grade, with the full support of Mom and Dad. He had odd jobs, but never a career. It didn't seem a priority to him to escape a life of poverty. He accepted the lifestyle in which we were raised and was content with living his life the same way. Like a nomad, he jumped around from job to job and from one girlfriend to another, shunning responsibility almost with a passion. When he finally discovered his true calling in life, he became a Latin singer, and devoted his life to singing, mostly for charity, and for audiences in his neighborhood in New Britain, Connecticut.

My two sisters, Evelyn and Susan, also dropped out of school early, got married, and had children. They both stayed in the neighborhood where we grew up, or close enough to be within fifteen minutes of my parents' apartment. Susan still lives in the rented apartment where my parents lived before her on 94th Street in Jackson Heights, Queens. I used to think they were content with following the lifestyle in which we were raised. That was fine as long as they were happy. It was not, however, what I wanted for my life. If I was an exception among my siblings, so was my younger brother, Wil, who followed in my footsteps. He, like all of us, dropped out of high school, but went back and graduated. He had many of the aspirations that I did and looked up to me as a role model, something I did not have in either my dad or Nelson when I was growing up. I have always been pleased to have been his role model and inspiration. Wil made me very proud the day he graduated from New York University and became a successful professional in the technology field, the very same industry in which I built a successful career.

For my other siblings, it was as if they were stuck in quicksand and could not get out. They accepted that violence, poverty, and negativity were a part of who they were. The unfortunate part is that without the drive and hunger to elevate themselves from the impoverished lifestyle that was all too commonplace for all of us, it would very likely be repeated in future generations. Someone had to break the mold!

I decided to take the initiative to control my own life and not give in to the guilt I felt, or that my parents tried to make me feel, because I wanted to be different.

The violence that is fostered in the home at some point migrates into the street. That is mostly inevitable, except for a small percentage of inner-city youths who manage to get out—not unscathed necessarily, but out. They still have to deal with the memories of the way they were raised. I am always amazed when I hear news reports of violence in the inner-city neighborhoods. Violence occurs so frequently that it isn't even news anymore, and hasn't been for many years.

A news outlet will report the violence, and people automatically wonder why one person robs from another or kills another human being. They tend to blame the "street" life, or poor schooling, or an impoverished life. Unfortunately, very rarely is anything done early enough in the lives of our youths to ensure that they are provided with a strong foundation from the time they are toddlers—at home. This tragedy is often passed down for generations, until someone makes the difficult decision to break the pattern. It is only then that a new and positive pattern can take the family down a different path.

I remember getting a call from a family member about twelve years ago. She informed me that a cousin was stabbed to death in a dispute at the grocery store downstairs from where Susan lived and still lives today. The murder was not reported on any news network. The 115th Precinct is only two blocks from where the murder took place.

By that time I had succeeded in getting out of the neighborhood and away from the family, and I was living in New Jersey. It was something I felt I had to do to find my own identity away from the temptations of the old neighborhood. I broke the pattern of our history.

My cousin was perhaps twenty years old when his life was taken from him over something that was not worth the tragic loss of anyone's life. But, he was hanging out in the wrong place with the wrong people. It was a place where street pride and the display of superiority are more important than life itself. These were young people hanging out in the streets late at night, passing the time doing nothing productive, just hanging out. It's almost as if they were stray kids. The police didn't give it much attention. It was just another inner-city tragedy, another statistic. The killer was identified as an illegal immigrant.

Another cousin promised he would avenge the killing. An eye for an eye, or more appropriately, a life for a life seemed justifiable. Some in the family actually expected (almost demanded) quick revenge and were disappointed when weeks went by and the killer was still living in the neighborhood, not even arrested. It was only a matter of time before his life was snuffed out, vengeance taken!

There is no question that it is extremely complicated and challenging to recognize the effort required to be different, to break the vicious cycle of negativity, and work continuously and with laser-like focus to be a positive, progressive, and successful human being. But, imagine what impact it will have on future generations. It takes the first one to attend college. Then another. Perhaps a younger sibling follows that new example and does the same. They have children who attend college. And on and on!

My challenge involved going against the grain of the family lifestyle, and that was not easy. The first one to break the mold must have the bravery of a pioneer. My efforts to improve my own life and my living standard were viewed as egotistical and elitist. The pressure to accept the patterns that were passed down for generations rather than veer in a more progressive direction was at times intense. It made me question if I was doing the right thing. Even with the doubt and guilt that I felt as a result of my parents' reaction to my efforts to ultimately escape a life of poverty, something inside me was stronger and made sure I stayed the course. Maybe it was youthful stubbornness that motivated me to resist the pressure my parents put on me. Fortunately, I was able to persevere with a dogged determination to transform my life. I was compelled to go with my instincts and not permit my past to dictate my future.

As a teenager I often experienced sadness that my parents could not get us out of poverty and that we could not have a happier, more pleasant home. Perhaps it was the constant pressure they felt as they struggled to pay the rent and put food on the table for five kids. Following in their own parents' footsteps, they wanted to have a large family, where Dad goes to work and Mom stays home to care for the house and the kids.

It seemed like my journey to reach the point where I could say I was finally out of an impoverished environment was a lifelong one. I was constantly looking in the mirror and questioning my actions and my mistakes along the way. It was through that constant self-examination that I was able to make adjustments in my strategy and direction, often aided by constructive experiences with mentors and friendships I developed through the years.

I'm a big believer that to be true to yourself and be a genuine human being, you must be willing and able to be reflective of your own behavior; you must be your own best (not worst) critic.

It is by employing through the years that practice of self-criticism that I have been able to refine how I treat others and how I conduct my own life's affairs. But in spite of all the improvements I have labored diligently to make in my life, the one thing I have not been able to do is release the many angry, sad memories of childhood.

The real basis of this book is to bring more light to how parents can damage children's lives with negative, destructive, even abusive behavior, when what they should be doing is teaching them, mentoring them to be good, productive, sharing, and loving human beings. And how we can overcome the negative baggage and avoid passing it down to future generations.

It is the latter that plants the seeds for a child to develop a strong foundation with a healthy self-esteem, self-confidence, and the willingness to take initiative as opportunities present themselves, without the fear of rejection and ridicule.

My recollection of events goes way back to when I was as young as five years old, in 1962.

Chapter One

We were living in the South Bronx on 179th Street near the train station where the IRT number 5 train stopped, Tremont Avenue, with an exit toward the front of the platform on 179th Street. Our building was between Vyse Avenue and Boston Road. We lived there for probably four years, in an apartment with two bedrooms and one bathroom. Five of us kids slept in one bedroom, and my parents were in the other one.

Wherever we lived up to the time I was sixteen years old, the five of us kids shared one bedroom. All seven of us, including my parents, always shared one bathroom.

We were three boys and two girls, each two years apart for at least part of the year. All of us were born in the summer months, except for my younger brother Wil, who was born in November. I was the second oldest behind Nelson.

In the Bronx I grew up playing in the street from an early age. At five years old I spent much of the day outside in front of the building where we lived, usually throwing a Spalding rubber ball against the wall of the building across the street from ours. I chose that building to play catch against because it was the most level part of the street. The street was uphill, but less so toward the bottom of the street where we lived.

My mom would usually keep an eye on me by leaning out the window, when she wasn't cooking or caring for my brothers and sisters. That was usually her entertainment, as was common in the city. During the summer many people in the neighborhood sought relief from the heat by hanging out of their windows, or sitting on their fire escapes, which was our version of a terrace.

Back then we called my mom Mami and my dad Papi. We spoke Spanglish at home, a mixture of Spanish and English—standard practice for Puerto Ricans. Mom came to New York in 1948 at the age of twelve, two years after my grandfather Julio settled in the Bronx and sent for the rest of the family. Dad arrived in New York at the age of fifteen in 1946. He too settled in the South Bronx, coincidentally not far from where Mom would live two years later. Like many of the Puerto Ricans who migrated to the mainland during those days, my parents proudly held on to their island lifestyle and heritage, never learning to speak English very well.

One day as I was playing outside, Mom called for me from our apartment window. I was across the street and a little bit west of our apartment, so I had to look left in the direction that traffic was coming from in order to see her on the window ledge. I had to cross the street to get to our side of 179th Street, a one-lane street with cars parked on either side. I was five years old, and not tall enough to see above two cars that were double-parked. I tried to be careful crossing the street, and had to lean forward from the front of one of the double-parked cars to check for any approaching cars.

As I leaned forward, I saw a car speeding up the street. It was coming so fast that when the driver saw me, he pressed his brakes and the tires screeched as he came to a stop. He must have thought I was going to cross the street. He was going so fast that he ended up stopping probably two or three car lengths up the hill beyond where I was standing. Mom, who was still looking out the window, started yelling hysterically, thinking the worst was about to happen to me. She panicked and so was unable to warn me about the nearing car.

Anyway, the driver got out of his car and asked if I was okay. It turns out that the front bumper of the car grazed my right knee, which was sticking out from behind the double-parked car. It didn't really hurt, but it scared me. The driver was also scared, and Mom was hysterical upstairs.

I hesitated before finally crossing the street and hurried up to our apartment as my heart pounded against my chest. When I got upstairs, Mom was still screaming. On the one hand, she was asking me if I was okay. She wanted to make sure nothing happened to me. On the other hand, she was frightening me by screaming and acting hysterical. I was so afraid of her reaction that I went and hid behind one of the beds in the cramped bedroom that I shared with my brothers and sisters.

My mom came into the room, found me hiding behind the farthest bed from the door, and proceeded to beat on me. I suppose that was her way of communicating to me that at five years old I should know better than to nearly get killed by a car which was speeding up the street. Somehow she felt that it was my fault.

The beating caused me much more physical pain than the accident with the car. The emotional pain, the fear as I hid behind the bed in anticipation of what was coming, was also much worse. I was taught at an early age that if something went wrong in my life, it must have been my fault.

That minor accident, although it could have been much worse, happened so quickly that I didn't have much time to be frightened. Sure I was afraid, but that came and went in a flash. Mom's reaction actually made it worse in many respects. It made it difficult for me at such a young age to confide in her whenever something negative happened to me. It began to teach me to resist sharing information with her, whether it was a fight with another kid, a negative encounter with an adult, or an accident in the street.

There was no praise for avoiding a potentially fatal accident by peeking out from behind the double-parked car. Had I just run across the street, as a spontaneous reaction to Mom calling for me, I probably would not be here today to tell this story.

It wasn't long after that incident that I saw another neighborhood kid killed by a speeding car on the very same street. I saw the car speeding up 179th Street, and then suddenly slamming into a kid who was running across the street. The boy, who I did not know, flew in the air and landed near the sidewalk, his head smashing onto the concrete sidewalk and his body landing on the pavement.

A fire department truck was nearby and hurried to the scene. The firemen tried to help the boy by placing one of their jackets under his head to provide some support to his badly injured head. As they waited for an ambulance, the boy moaned in pain, but wasn't moving. Before the ambulance arrived on the scene, the boy stopped moaning and he was gone. I'll never forget that unfortunate incident. It always made me think about my car accident. The same thing could have happened to me had I just run across the street when Mom called me.

I've always wondered why Mom reacted with such panic, rather than using that, or any other mishap, as an opportunity to teach me something positive. It would have been much more productive if she had used that experience to teach me how to better handle a similar situation in the future. She could have instructed me to walk down to the corner and cross at the intersection. This would have given me a better view of oncoming traffic, and cars could clearly see me, rather than crossing in the middle of the block with double-parked cars in the way.

That, however, would have been counter to her thinking. Since my parents' approach was to take the easy way out of things, crossing the street in the middle of the block, even for a five-year-old, made perfect sense to Mom. I just needed to make sure I didn't get hit by a car.

It was the combination of my near accident and witnessing that boy get killed that drilled in me how to be careful when crossing the street. Even today, some fifty years later, the scene of that boy being thrown through the air, moaning for a few minutes, and then going silent and motionless is indelibly engraved in my memory. I wished that I was able to help him, but no one could. It was too late for him. I could tell that even the firemen who were crouched over him felt helpless as they whispered, "You are going to be okay, you are going to be okay."

At the early and tender age of five, I was learning that I was responsible for anything that went wrong, and if my parents saw or heard that I did something they considered wrong or a mistake, I would be subjected to a beating for it.

My parents just didn't have the necessary foresight to be aware of the trauma they were causing. Nor could they consider what effect their treatment of me might cause decades later.

It was common for either Mom or Dad to beat me with a broom, coat hangers, belts, or rubber hoses. They would grab me by the hand and hold me while whipping me around my legs with a belt. I reacted by jumping up and down, trying to get away. I thought that somehow if I jumped, I could avoid having the belt hit me as directly as if I just stood there. I was a kid trying to find a way to protect myself—from my parents.

If I made them even angrier by running away and hiding to avoid a beating, the result was my being whipped with the buckle of my dad's belt. The physical abuse was always preceded by verbal abuse. The words they used were bad enough to destroy any kid's self-esteem and trust in his parents. In retrospect, they did not know or consider the damage they were causing us kids or me in particular. I can only guess that the violence with which they reacted and the trauma and pain they inflicted on their children was something they learned from their parents, but I have always been puzzled by this notion because I never saw any evidence of that in either of my maternal or paternal grandparents. I wonder if my parents ever felt a sense of guilt or remorse for doing the things they did to us. Did one say to the other as they lay in bed at night, "I wish I hadn't done that"?

I learned pretty quickly though that the best thing to do was to keep things hidden from them, in the interest of avoiding physical pain. There were many occasions over the years in which my parents abused or tormented me, but I was able to avoid a good many other potential beatings by not letting them know of things I did, or things that had happened to me.

The second time I was hit by a car was when I was six years old. I never told my parents about that accident. It's possible that since they didn't witness it themselves, I would not have been beaten, but I wasn't going to take that risk. It was the summer of 1963 and I was walking down the block consumed in utter summer boredom. When you're a kid and you're bored, invariably you seek some excitement, some adventure, to get your juices flowing.

I knew of a candy factory nearby where some other kids and I used to go for free candy. The factory's loading dock had trucks filled with boxes of candy. They had all kinds of lollipops and hard candies. Occasionally, we snuck into the factory lot by climbing through some openings in the chain-link fence that surrounded the property. We climbed on the back of the trucks, whose doors were unlocked, and helped ourselves to the candy.

On that particular hot summer day, I went into the lot alone, squeezed through the broken fence, and climbed on the back of a truck. The hot sun made the candy somewhat sticky, but I grabbed as much of it as I could carry. I didn't take a box, thinking that it would be too bulky to get through the fence and would only slow me down in my escape. So I just grabbed whatever I could bundle up in my arms and close to my body. I started running to get home as quickly as I could. I ran up 179th Street, a block away from our apartment, near the corner of what I think is Bryant Avenue today.

All of a sudden, I was on the ground, partially underneath the front of a car. I was not badly hurt, luckily, but I recall that my candies had flown all over the street.

When I looked up I saw that the car that hit me was a station wagon driven by an elderly person. The station wagon was a cream color with wood trim on the sides, vintage 1960s. The driver looked like he was old enough to be a grandfather. A woman, who I assumed was his wife, was in the passenger seat. The strange thing was that there I was, this six-year-old kid lying in the street, and they didn't even get out of their car to check on me. I thought maybe they were so scared, they didn't want to stick around. Still, I thought they should have gotten out and checked if I was okay.

The accident happened just outside of the *bodega*, a Spanish grocery store, which was on the corner. The guys in the bodega knew me because my family went there regularly for things like milk and bread. There was always a small contingent of local men hanging out there with the store owner and his assistant. They passed the time chatting, watching sports on a small television set, and drinking beers. There was one man who always ate bananas. He didn't drink beer, but he was meticulous in how he peeled the whole banana. He stood there and peeled away the entire skin, and then he peeled every string from the body. Only then did he begin eating the banana.

When the guys in the store heard the accident, some of them went outside to see what had happened. I was still lying in the street, more scared than hurt, when the guys saw me, a neighborhood kid, hurt on the ground, and the car driving away. One of the guys went into the bodega, grabbed a machete, and two of them began chasing the car. I don't think they ever caught up with the driver, but I was not going to stick around to see if they did. I got up off the ground, recovered as many of my candies as I could, and continued home.

My parents never knew about this accident. They never even asked where I got all the candy. They were just glad that I had candy and could share with my brothers and sisters. Luckily for me, the guys at the bodega never mentioned anything to them either.

If Mom had found out that I stole the candy and also got hit by a car, she would have beaten me. Since she was also a devout Catholic (which I always thought was ironic), she would have at minimum admonished me with a religious warning. She might have told me that the car accident was God's punishment for stealing the candy. My dad would not have cared. He beat me for things that happened around the house, or if we were out on the street somewhere and I made him upset. He was always pretty grumpy. I don't ever remember him saying "I love you" to any of us or hugging us. He was pretty weird that way. He definitely inherited that from his mom.

My paternal grandmother was also very grumpy. Come to think of it, both my grandmothers were grumpy. I didn't think they were very nice. My grandfathers, on the other hand, were warm and friendly. My maternal grandfather was alive when the first edition of this book was written last year, but he passed away in January 2015. He was 103 years and eight months of age. Julio Vicente was a wonderful man and a loving grandfather.

Being six years old and already afraid of my parents, I began to withdraw from communicating with them, as much as a six-year-old can. I tried not to share any details with them about who I was playing with outside, where I was playing, or if I got into a fight at school. I just assumed that telling them might get me into trouble. Still, there was much trouble that lay ahead.

Chapter Two

In September of 1963 I entered school for the first time. It was at PS 6, at the corner of Vyse and Tremont Avenues, that Mom enrolled me for the first grade. Just about two months into that first year at school, I was shaken by an event that, unknown to me at the time, had worldwide implications. Although I could not comprehend the monumental impact, I knew that it frightened and saddened me. With a perceptibly simple announcement over the school's public address system on the afternoon of November 22, 1963, a woman informed the entire school that President John F. Kennedy had been assassinated. She also announced that due to the tragedy the school was closing early that day. All my classmates were in disbelief, wondering why someone would assassinate the president. I imagine all the adults were just as upset as they struggled to make sense of the terrible crime.

The woman's delivery of the news, with a voice that reflected sadness and pain, was enough to make me feel unhappy and frightened. That message was delivered after our lunch break and before we were scheduled to have recess for exercise. We were released for the day and I had to walk home alone.

Back then, there were no phone calls made to parents to pick up their kids when they were released early. We were city kids and accustomed to being outside by ourselves. Once we were dismissed, I hurried home, walking as quickly as I could to cover the three blocks to our apartment.

As I walked home, all I could think of was the chill I felt all over my body. It had nothing to do with the late fall weather, but rather the fear that the recent news caused. I had no idea what it meant or why the president would be assassinated, so I started thinking maybe I would be killed also. I was afraid of even entering our apartment building alone. I remember thinking that someone could grab me and kill me in the darkened hallway. As soon as I got into our apartment, I was so afraid that I crouched behind a chair in our living room as the goose bumps slowly disappeared.

Mom was watching the news, as I imagine everyone was, trying to find out the details of what happened to our president. Dad was working and I don't remember when he got home that day.

That event had a big impact on me, and is one I remember quite vividly. Although it made me gloomy and scared, I never spoke to my parents about how I felt, and they never asked. They never explained why someone would want to have our president assassinated. We did watch the news together and that was how I gathered information about the manner in which the president died.

With the news on the television seemingly nonstop, I watched the constant replaying of the president slumping over Jacqueline Kennedy after being shot in the head as his motorcade traveled in Dallas, Texas. I saw Jackie climbing briefly on top of the back of the convertible as a Secret Service officer seemed to push the car forward, then climbed on the back to help Jackie and the president. It was not exactly rated for young children to see, but I even saw when Lee Harvey Oswald was shot by Jack Ruby as the police were walking him past reporters.

I was an impressionable kid, and that event added to my becoming cautious and suspicious of people in general.

Sometime during the summer of 1964, when I was seven years old, I started becoming interested in baseball. We had one of those televisions covered in wood furniture. The television was in our living room, so I often sat on the floor there and watched the Yankees play. I watched ballplayers like Mickey Mantle, Tom Tresh, Roger Maris, Joe Pepitone, Jake Gibbs, Elston Howard, Jim Bouton, Whitey Ford, Steve Hamilton, Al Downing, and many others. These were baseball players who, as a young kid, I idolized. I thought they had the greatest life. They spent their days outside in the ballpark, playing a sport they loved.

I remember thinking how cool Joe Pepitone was, with all that hair that always seemed perfectly combed, saturated with hair spray to keep it in place. I don't know how he kept his cap on. Steve Hamilton I remember because he used to throw this high blooper pitch that most batters could never hit. It was so comical to see the batters wait, for what seemed to be forever, for the pitch to get to the plate, swing desperately, and either miss it entirely or awkwardly foul it off. I remember the announcers laughing every time he threw that pitch and they saw the batters swing and miss. I remember Al Downing as a pitcher because his birthday was one day before mine, on June 28.

I liked all the Yankees, but my favorites were Mantle and Maris. They were the power of the team back then, and they were fun to watch. Whether I was watching them on the television or at the ballpark, it made me want to be a baseball player.

Dad took me to games at Yankee Stadium on occasional weekends, and we sat in the bleachers in center field. The weather was always extremely hot, with the sun right in our faces, but I didn't care. I was out there watching my idols play. I could see Mickey Mantle right below us in center field flirting with some ladies in between innings. I could walk to the end of the section where we sat and lean over the railing and see who was warming up in the Yankees bullpen. In the old stadium it was in the right field section of the stadium.

My favorite time was when Dad took me to the stadium on either ball day or bat day. It was always so cool to come home with a shiny ball or bat. I dreaded the first time they got scuffed up, but I loved my bats and balls. On one ball day, once we got to our seats I asked him, "Papi, can I go downstairs?"

"Okay, but hurry back," he said.

"Thanks, Papi. Here, hold my ball for me." I went to the usher handing out the balls at one of the entrance gates and told him I had not gotten a ball. I was thrilled to go home with two baseballs.

Once we went on cap day and I came home with my new Yankees cap and an idea. I had a cap, but no uniform. I begged Mom to get me a Yankees uniform until she finally took me to a sporting goods store on Tremont Avenue that was within walking distance for us, maybe six blocks away. The uniform she bought me was the visitors' gray with the New York logo on the front. Since it had no number on the back, I got a black marker and wrote in the number 9. First I traced the outline and then filled it in with the same marker. I could tell that it wasn't as perfect as a sewn-in number, but it was good enough. Now I had my Roger Maris uniform.

I took one of my shiny baseballs, a mitt that someone must have given me, and went outside to play. I had not started playing any type of organized team sports yet, and I didn't have any friends with whom to play baseball, but I learned to throw and catch. All I could do was throw my ball against the brick wall of the building across the street and catch it with my mitt as it came back to me. I remember being hot and sweaty in my uniform and wondering how the Yankee players could stand playing out in the sun with uniforms that were so hot and heavy. But I kept playing catch against the brick wall. I was quite happy pretending to be a baseball player. At that time, and for years that followed, it was truly all I wanted to do.

I was out there only a few minutes when one throw got away from me and broke a window on the first floor of the apartment building. I got so scared that I turned and ran back up to our apartment. I didn't say anything to Mom, of course. But the superintendent of that building must have seen me, because she knocked on our door to inform Mom of what had happened. She told her that she had to pay for the window replacement.

Mom did not see this as an accident by a seven-year-old who lost his grip and perhaps should not be throwing a hard baseball against a brick wall from the middle of the street. It didn't occur to her that maybe she should find a way to take me to the park a few blocks away to play catch there with Nelson, or find some friends to play catch with. Instead, she saw it as a mistake I made that was going to cost her and Dad money they didn't have, and I should be punished for it. She found me hiding behind the bed and beat me while she screamed at me.

I think she was embarrassed that the superintendent complained to her. That humiliation and the anger that I caused her made her beat me.

Chapter Three

Mom was twenty-one when I was born on June 29, 1957. By the time she was twenty-eight, she had five children ranging in age from nine to one. Dad was five years her senior.

When he was seventeen years old, Dad enlisted in the United States Army. He served for three years during the Korean War and was deployed abroad in Pusan, Korea. He spent one year and three days there, where hard-pressed American, South Korean, and United Nations forces were desperately hanging onto the southeast tip of the Korean peninsula. Dad was trained as a medical technician and, when deployed, became a member of Medical Detachment 704, for which he proudly earned a Combat Medical Badge. He was awarded the CMB for his service in accompanying infantrymen into the demilitarized zone between North and South Korea. He was also decorated with the Korean Presidential Citation and the Korean Service Medal.

He never spoke to us about his experiences in the war, so we never really knew what he did, until many years later. I always wanted to know if he saw combat action and if he killed any enemy soldiers. Mom sometimes joked that all he did was peel potatoes in the war. I never thought her jokes about his time in the war were funny, but Dad always laughed at them. I would have been very proud of him if I had known as a young boy what his military experience was like. I think Mom was just jealous because Dad had a tattoo on his left arm of "Mary," a girlfriend he had while stationed in Korea.

When we lived in the Bronx, Dad was a factory worker for the Sunshine Biscuits Company. He worked nights, so each day he departed from home in the afternoon and returned around one in the morning. After he got home from work, he slept until about eleven in the morning. He was not around to play with us unless it was the weekend. It wasn't his nature to be playful with us kids anyway. Most weekends he sat around the living room watching baseball on television. I was luckier than my other siblings because I was the one he always took to the games at Yankee Stadium on the weekends when he could afford it. He was an avid Yankees fan. That was our time to bond as father and son. I thought he was happiest when he was at the stadium, sitting with me in the bleachers, with a beer cup in his hand.

We always sat in the bleachers, except for one memorable occasion. Someone had given him box seat tickets to a Yankees game. When we got to the stadium, I expected us to make our usual visit to the box office so Dad could buy our bleacher seat tickets, which at the time cost seventy-five cents each. That one time, however, he told me that he had the tickets already. He led me to a different section and showed me to our seats. I couldn't believe that he and I were sitting directly behind home plate. He was beaming at the opportunity to treat me to a game in "luxury" seats. While it was a thrill for me as well, I actually felt I had a better view of the entire field from the bleachers. I never told that to Dad, of course. I knew that the box seats were a one-time occurrence and I didn't want to be disrespectful or unappreciative. After that game, we were back in the bleachers, which I actually liked and preferred.

Even though Dad didn't play with us kids as a matter of routine, one weekend day we all went as a family to a park for a picnic. Dad and I took baseball mitts and a ball, and played catch. That was a tremendous highlight for me because it was the one time that we had gone to a park as a family. Usually, it was Mom who took us all to a park, the Bronx Zoo, or to Orchard Beach. I was so excited to be able to show him that I knew how to catch a baseball. It didn't matter if he threw me a short hop or one high over my head: I was going to catch it. I wanted to show him that I had a skill and that he could be proud of me. I was so happy, it didn't matter to me that he was throwing so hard that I hurt my hand. I must have bent my thumb backward when catching one of his hard throws. He never noticed because I refused to wince or show pain in any way. I just sucked it in and kept throwing and catching with my dad. I remember him telling Mom to look at how well I could catch and throw a baseball.

Every now and then he would show pride in some-thing I did, though he was not one to tell me directly that he was proud of me. Once when we were at a Yankees game, he told a drinking buddy he met at the game that he should hear how I could whistle. I had learned to whistle loudly from a boy Mom used to babysit for. He must have spent two days teaching me. Even when his mom picked him up and took him home, I practiced endlessly. Finally when the whistle came out through my tongue and lips, I was ecstatic. I whistled all day long it seemed. I showed Mom and then Dad when he was home from work. My whistle was loud enough to hail a cab!

So at the ballgame, Dad said, "Fatty, show him how you whistle." I was a little embarrassed, but whistled as my dad asked. I wasn't sure the man was impressed, but Dad was and that was all that mattered to me. It felt good to know I made him proud.

At that early age, I was the only athletic kid in the family. Nelson never cared for sports, and my younger brother, Wil, was too young then at only three. In later years though, he became a good athlete.

Even after we returned home from the park, I never mentioned a thing about my injured hand. Eventually, it just healed on its own. The funny thing is that over the years playing baseball, I would re-injure that same hand, usually when sliding into a base. But at the time it first happened, I didn't care about anything other than showing Dad what a talented ballplayer I was.

With Mom busy with the five kids and Dad working to support a family of seven on a factory salary, there was no time to guide or mentor me in becoming a baseball player. My parents were the type to live hand to mouth. They did just enough to get by one day at a time. There was never any planning and they seemingly never aspired to reach a higher standard of living.

Consequently, they never enrolled us kids into any type of organized event. I would have loved to play Little League baseball and then move up from there. The only organized thing we did was go to school. I guess it was only because it was mandatory. It's what kids had to do. That made me envious of friends in the neighborhood whose parents took them to play Little League baseball.

Neither of my parents drove a car or had a driver's license, so we always rode the subway or buses wherever we went. They never had a checkbook or a bank account for long-term savings. If they had a savings account, it would be for a short period of time, maybe a few months. They did not live by the concept of preparing us for tomorrow. They just wanted to live day by day, and hoped we five children would grow up to be just like them.

The summer of 1965, I turned eight years old. My birthday that year was like all the previous ones that I could remember. I was out on the street playing baseball, walking around the Bronx River with some friends, wrestling on the sidewalk, or stealing candy from the nearby candy factory's trucks. I wonder why they never locked those trucks. My parents never celebrated my birthday with a party or gave me a card. There was never a birthday cake.

That summer I was walking alone up 179th Street from the bodega and saw Mom walking toward me with Nelson and Evelyn. I remember being excited to see them and thinking we were going somewhere for my birthday. I walked faster to meet them and asked Mom where we were going. She told me they were going to the World's Fair.

That's right, "they" were going. I had no idea what the World's Fair was, of course, but I wanted to go with them. I absolutely assumed I was going with them. I mean, how could Mom go somewhere and not take me as well, especially on my birthday? Maybe she thought I was independent because I was always outside playing alone. Perhaps she didn't have enough money for one more. Maybe she didn't want me with her. That's how I really felt back then…that she did not want me.

I never got over the pain of being left behind with no good explanation as to why. It just made no sense to me. Over the years, this type of disappointment occurred time and again. I believe that is why I became more and more independent. I believe it is also why I grew to resent my parents. I figured I needed to take care of myself if I wanted to survive and thrive.

Chapter Four

The next year we moved to a different apartment only a few blocks away and closer to my school. Our apartment was one of two street-level apartments that stood on either side of the building entrance. It was a five- or six-story building shaped like a U, with an entrance courtyard. I thought our street-level apartment was nice because we could open the windows and see through the screens right out into the street. It was great in the summer, although we had to be careful to close the windows when the kids opened the fire hydrant across the street to get some relief from the heat. If they gushed water like a fire hose through a soda or beer can opened on both ends, we might get wet.

I was always an early riser and the first one in our home to wake up. I was impatient and did not want to sleep late. I wanted to do things. I wanted to play baseball or stickball, and spin tops or play skelly in the middle of the street. This was the 1960s, so there were no computer games, only street games in the Bronx. We were active kids and had the time of our lives.

I typically was out in the street by seven in the morning, practicing spinning my top in the middle of the street or teaching myself to chop off the tops of soda bottles against the top of a fire hydrant to use in a game of skelly. It wasn't easy because more often than not the bottle top cracked and broke. If it did not break initially, it could fall to the ground and then break. It was a delicate task. It was a real art to chop it off cleanly and catch it.

Using the bottle tops instead of the bottle caps was cool because the glass made them glide more smoothly in the skelly box that was painted in the middle of the street. They also slid a longer distance. The bottle caps were much stronger though because they were filled with wax or tar, which we scraped off the street when the hot sun softened it. It turned the game into one of finesse, with the smooth, shiny glass tops against strength, with the wax or tar-filled bottle caps.

By the time other kids got up to play, I was ready. Sometimes we played stickball in the street using a manhole cover as second base. We used thick white chalk to draw first and third base on the asphalt beside parked cars. Another manhole cover served as home plate. The bat we used was usually a cutoff broomstick. The highlight was when we were able to afford a stickball bat from the corner candy store. It was a thick, shiny stick that was well sanded, polished, and taped around the top, to give you a good grip. If we didn't have a stick, we simply played punch-ball.

One afternoon Mom was preparing dinner, and all of us kids were running around the apartment playing. Our play extended into the kitchen, where Mom was cooking. I don't remember what we were playing, but we were being noisy. That is what kids who are ten, eight, six, four, and two do.

Usually when Mom was cooking, I was in the kitchen sampling her food. She gladly gave me either an olive or a piece of meat or some potatoes with broth if she was making *carne guisada*, beef stew. All our food was typical Puerto Rican food, usually rice and beans, fried plantains, and a meat or fish. On truly special days we had steamed blue crabs (which we all loved!) with our rice and beans. Dad brought them home alive from the market in a double brown paper bag. Mom was a very good cook, so we enjoyed our meals.

That afternoon though, we were busy running and playing. At one point, she must have asked us to stop and we didn't. We just kept on playing. I mean, it was maybe five in the afternoon. What else could we do besides being rambunctious? But something set her off in the worst way. She yelled at us and suddenly picked up a large kitchen knife. We all got scared and ran into the bathroom. In the apartment, like all others that we had lived in, we had one bathroom to share among the seven of us. We were terrified, thinking she was going to kill one or all of us. She actually chased us to the bathroom, where we locked ourselves in.

The old building had solid doors and concrete walls, so she could not smash the door down or bust open the lock. There was no sheetrock to stab through. It must have frustrated her even more that she could not get to any of us. It was as if she was possessed with evil intentions.

She continued screaming, telling us she was going to kill us. We could hear and feel the point of the knife puncturing the solid door. She must have stabbed at the door four or five times. This lasted for what felt like an eternity. Eventually, she stopped stabbing at the door and screaming. But we stayed in the bathroom, too afraid to come out. I was sure that if we opened the door, she was going to stab some of us. When Mom was enraged it was as if she was under some spell.

After about ten minutes we opened the door and slowly ventured out. We were all very quiet as we tippy-toed into the hallway between the bathroom and the living room. My brothers and sisters went into the living room and turned on the television. I quietly walked into the kitchen, where Mom had resumed cooking. This was the worst, up to that point, that we had seen her. I suddenly felt that she was capable of killing any of us. We survived that nightmare, but not unscathed. Imagine the damage that type of reaction can cause young children. Nothing good can come from that.

My mother would become so enraged that she would lose total control. Now that I think about it, I can't imagine what five children can do to make a parent frighten them so much and threaten their lives with that kind of response to their being rowdy. After the episode was over, there was never a word said about it. There was no apology or explanation of the event. Dinner was served as if nothing had happened, though Mom was menacingly silent. It's a good thing that her cooking was good because we were going to eat it whether we liked it or not. We ate dinner and kept an eye on where the kitchen knives were.

She never said anything to make us feel like she regretted doing that to us or assured us that she would never hurt us with a knife. Nothing was ever mentioned to Dad when he returned home from work that night, or the next day, or ever.

It was strange and scary to see the stab marks on the bathroom door as a constant reminder all the years that we lived there—from the time I was eight to the day before I turned twelve years old. Even if Mom's intention was just to scare us into behaving, it was certainly not the way to teach children a lesson. The only things we learned from that experience were fear, anger, hate, and violence. Mom didn't stab any of us, but the episode left deep wounds.

It was another lesson that encouraged me to stay away from my parents as much as possible. The streets were my diversion until I could break away completely. I spent more time outside playing than inside the apartment. When I wasn't playing I was doing things like helping a neighbor wash his car. He paid me twenty-five cents and I'm sure he did that to be nice and to teach me the value of doing some work for pay.

This turned out to be another valuable outlet for me. My parents didn't have money to spare, so if I asked them for a quarter or a dime, they usually said no. Mom was more giving than Dad, though. Sometimes she asked him for change and gave it to me. She knew that if I asked him directly, he was bound to say no, just for the sake of not saying yes. Sometimes he got angry with me for asking and slapped me on my head. He especially did that if we were out at the supermarket. He did not like being asked for money.

Dad regularly took me with him to do the weekly grocery shopping each Thursday, which was payday for him. Mom stayed home with my brothers and sisters. She never went to the supermarket. Dad had two qualities that I always disliked. He was cheap and he was grumpy. I guess he had many other qualities that I disliked because he was violent enough that I tried to stay away from him. He never seemed happy. It was confusing for me—one day he would be slapping me in public for asking for some change, and on the weekend he would take me to Yankee Stadium to watch a game.

Although the bleacher seats at Yankee Stadium back then cost only seventy-five cents and the subway token was a dime, Dad spent more money getting tipsy with beer and springing for a hot dog or peanuts for me. It's difficult to comprehend today that there was a time when a father and son could enjoy a baseball game live for all of maybe ten bucks!

Back at home and behind the closed doors of our cramped apartment, we didn't always enjoy the bonding that Dad and I shared at the ball park. The home routine was more chaotic. Whenever Mom or Dad got angry with me, I ended up running to hide from a beating. Often I hid under a bed in our bedroom. I thought, incorrectly, that if they didn't see me, they could not get to me. But while

Mom waited with belt in hand, Dad poked me with a broomstick to get me out from under the bed. Mom never crawled on the floor to try to get me out. She left that to Dad.

First he stopped in the kitchen to pick up a broom. Then he knelt in front of the bed, where he proceeded to poke me with the broomstick, hard enough that the pain nudged me farther away from him. As I tried to avoid being poked, Mom grabbed me from the other end and I was forced out. The beating with the belt was prolonged by her anger at my hiding to avoid her.

It never occurred to my parents that my siblings and I hid because we were afraid. We never knew how bad the beatings were going to be. They could not consider that growing up afraid and subjected to violence was only going to make us violent, paranoid, untrusting, and generally stressed adults. After all, violence as a reaction to almost any mistake was normal to us.

Sometimes Mom used Dad's belt buckle to beat me with when she was wildly angry. Whenever she beat me with the buckle, scars developed on my legs. Come to think of it, she often went for my legs and not my arms. Sometimes she hit my back. I cried and squirmed and screamed for her to stop. If I tried to run into another room, it angered her so much that she had to chase me, and the result was that I got hit more.

By the time the beating was over, I just lay there and cried. It never made sense to me that my parents had to treat us that way. What could I possibly do to deserve that punishment? Our home wasn't founded on a practice of mentoring us kids and teaching us right from wrong. It was simply based on heavy punishment if we did something perceived to be wrong.

It was a vicious and ridiculous circle. If I fought with another kid at school and the school reported it to Mom, I got a beating for that. Yet, Mom was reinforcing in me the practice of violence as the repercussion or punishment of a misdeed. Naturally, if a kid at school did something I viewed as wrong—take a pencil from me, bump me on the lunch line—my reaction was not only to hit him, but to beat him so he could not retaliate.

No one in our extended family ever had any knowledge of the violence that was all too normally a part of our household. Not my grandparents and not any of my ten aunts and uncles—all on Mom's side of the family. We were fairly close as an extended family, visiting each other on a regular, weekly basis. We celebrated holidays together and enjoyed being around each other. Yet I never mentioned to anyone outside our home that my parents beat me the way they did. It actually seemed normal to me, even if I didn't like it. There was nothing to like or dislike. That was just the way it was.

Chapter Five

Although Nelson was not interested in athletics, one day he decided to join my friends and me in a game of punch-ball in the street just outside of our apartment on Vyse Avenue. On one play there was a kid running all the way from second base to home plate. Nelson was playing defense and stood his ground near home plate. Since he was not used to playing ball, he didn't know how to avoid contact while he waited for the throw. The kid running barreled into him and Nelson fell to the ground, banging his head pretty hard.

I could hear when his head hit the manhole cover. He must have been ten years old at the time. He lay on the ground for a few minutes, and he didn't cry or scream. I got pretty scared because he was just moaning and calling out for Mom. "Mommy, I'm dead, I'm dead," he repeated over and over again. A couple of kids helped me to stand him up and I walked him home, which was probably no more than fifty feet away.

I put him down on Mom's bed and explained what had happened. She was playing music and entertaining Gwee, a friend of hers. Mom was twenty-nine years old at that time. She didn't seem to think there was anything wrong with Nelson. I kept telling her that we needed to take him to the hospital. He hit his head on the manhole cover hard, and bounced up and down. She didn't want to cut short her socializing, so we never took him to the hospital.

Over the years, after that accident, Nelson was prone to doing some strange things, and he never developed into a responsible person. I always joked that it was because he hit his head on that manhole cover and as a result was simply not well.

I was angry at Mom for that because she didn't seem to care enough to at least have him checked out. I thought she should have interrupted the party and taken him to the hospital.

One summer Nelson got a job at the bodega around the corner from our apartment. He stocked shelves, filled the refrigerators with sodas and beer, swept the floors, and cleaned up. One day he came home with boxes of new toys. He was eleven years old and I was nine. Mom asked him where he got the toys. He told her that a friend's mom really liked him and took the two of them shopping and bought Nelson all the toys, including a shiny green bicycle. Mom, a bit gullible to say the least, was happy about that and asked to meet the friend's mom. Nelson said he thought that was a good idea and agreed to arrange for the two of them to meet.

After several alleged attempts to get the two moms, who had up to that moment never spoken to each other, to meet, Nelson informed Mom that the woman crushed her foot getting into her car and had to go to the hospital. As a result of that unfortunate accident, the two could not meet. Mom expressed concern for the woman and seemed to forget about the planned meeting. I guess she thought that the woman needed time to recover and there was no need to press for the meeting.

I was suspicious of Nelson's story, but didn't have any reason to suspect anything was wrong. But it seemed odd to me that some lady in the South Bronx would buy so many toys, and a bicycle, for a stranger of a boy. A day or two after Nelson had come home with all the toys, I walked into the bodega. The store owner was nice to me as he said hello. On this day, though, he asked where my brother Nelson was. He hadn't seen him in days. I told him he was at home. He invited me to go behind the counter and asked me if Nelson had a large sum of money.

I didn't understand the question until he showed me where, on a shelf on the wall behind the counter, normally stocked with cans of Goya beans, tomato sauce, and other foods, he had placed a small brown paper bag of dollar bills the last time Nelson worked at the store. He was going to deposit the money in the bank across the street, but got distracted and placed the bag on the shelf. Only he and Nelson had been behind the counter that afternoon when the bag of money disappeared. I didn't mention anything about the toys that a friend's mom allegedly bought Nelson, but I put the pieces together.

The store owner then invited me to the back room and had me stand beside him as he took practice shots into empty cardboard boxes with his gun. I guess he wanted me to let Nelson know that he had a gun and knew how to shoot it. He never threatened me with the pistol, but I got the message. It was a small gun and the shots sounded to me like firecrackers, except that they punctured holes in the boxes they hit. Nelson did not want to go back into that store again.

Nelson was clearly Mom's favorite child and was growing accustomed to getting away with most transgressions he committed. He was her first child from a previous marriage, so she always displayed a sentimental favoritism toward him. She was only nineteen when she gave birth to him. Nelson knew that he was Mom's favorite and felt he could stretch the boundaries with her. By the age of ten or so, he began to show in his behavior a propensity to lie, steal, and deceive, confident that he could convince Mom that whatever he did was forgivable, even acceptable. When she allowed him to get away with the episode with the toys, it served to reinforce and support the process of creating someone who would become a toxic individual. When he succeeded in getting away with taking the store owner's money and keeping all the toys he purchased with it, Nelson at that point knew that he could deceive Mom into getting, and doing, whatever he wanted. This only grew worse in the years that followed.

Even so, he was not exempt from her uncontrollable outbursts of violent rages. One afternoon, I walked into our apartment from playing outside and saw Mom strangling Nelson with a red rubber hose. She had the rubber hose around his neck as he stood on one of the beds in our bedroom screaming. She squeezed the hose and yelled at him, and I panicked. My instinct was to stop her before she killed him. I ran over and began screaming, asking her to stop. I tried to grab the hose, and eventually, I must have snapped her out of her raging trance and she stopped. Nelson was able to get away, gasping for air as he rubbed his neck.

My arrival at that moment was fortuitous in saving Nelson's life. No one else was in the house, so Mom's blind anger might have resulted in an unimaginable outcome. All too often we hear of stories on the evening news where a parent gets arrested for harming or killing a child and their immediate explanation is that they "didn't mean to do it." They were "just trying to discipline the child and things got out of control."

I never knew what precipitated that outburst of violence, and Nelson never mentioned any details to me. It was clear, however, that it was not a good idea for any of us to be alone with Mom. She had a susceptibility to tantrums that could be quite violent, and she never was one to apologize or to seek help. I think she might have been embarrassed to tell anyone about her violent and uncontrollable rages or to admit that she needed help. If I ever brought up an episode to her like strangling Nelson, she actually denied that she ever did such a thing.

Sometimes there were violent fights among other family members, which we kids had to witness. One evening there was a family party in our apartment with aunts and uncles on Mom's side of the family visiting. They all lived in different areas of the South Bronx and came over pretty often to have dinner, listen to salsa music, and have some drinks. The drinks of choice were usually beer or rum and Coke. I always enjoyed seeing my aunts, uncles, and cousins. At this one party, we had Rachel, Irma, Cookie, Robert, and William, who are some of my mom's brothers and sisters. Some came with their spouses or significant others. Rachel was fighting with her husband, David, so he did not accompany her on this occasion.

During the evening, David came by looking for his wife. David got loud when he was drunk, and he was drunk often. He knocked on the apartment door, but no one was willing to open it for him. He knew there were people there because of the lights and the loud music. No one tried to hide that from him, but they didn't want to let him in because Rachel didn't want to see him. Apparently, there was some marital friction between David and Rachel, and the family sided with their blood relation.

Eventually, David, drunk as he was, broke one of our windows. Two or three of my uncles and my dad ran outside and chased David around some cars. I followed behind them. It was a chaotic scene as David tried to run in his drunken stupor, wobbling more than running. The other men, a bit pasted themselves, chased him. It didn't take long for them to catch him, and when they did two of them held him while Dad punched him in the face. I was there watching this whole thing play out and was stunned.

David's nose was bleeding, and he was crying, saying that his nose was broken.

I had never seen Dad in a fight before. He wasn't violent that way outside the house. David was a small man, maybe five feet tall at most (Dad was seven inches taller), and very skinny, maybe a hundred pounds, so he didn't pose a physical threat to anyone. Plus, he was very drunk. They got him into our apartment to wash him up, and he was crying and moaning. Dad kept talking to him, trying to convince him that he wasn't the one who punched him in the face. "David, David, it wasn't me who hit you, right?" David was too drunk and confused over all the commotion to even remember who hit him.

The party was pretty much over at that point. My uncles and my dad tried to figure out how to patch the window before it could be repaired with new glass, and the ladies were consoling David and patching things up between him and Rachel. This one time David got what he wanted: he was in the apartment and with his wife. The two of them were always fighting, and eventually got divorced.

I recall that Rachel was living with some guy in an apartment in Newark, New Jersey. We called him Chino because, although he was Puerto Rican, his eyes were somewhat narrow and made him look Asian. Her two daughters went to live with her, and her son stayed behind with his dad. We lost touch with them for several years. Rachel and Chino are still together today. David passed away some years ago.

While living on Vyse Avenue, one night we all ran outside and to the apartment next door, which was on the opposite side of the building's courtyard entrance. We knew the neighbors; they had kids who were about the same age as Nelson and me. We used to go there for birthday parties. I remember that at one birthday party there I heard for the very first time the song "(I Can't Get

No) Satisfaction" by The Rolling Stones. I thought it was a cool song. I must have been ten years old then.

Mom, Nelson, and I ran over there late that one night after the woman who lived there rang our bell looking for help from Mom. It was about 10 p.m. and she was a bit hysterical. Her husband had shot himself in the head. I never got to actually see him, but that's what we were told. The ambulance took him away and I never saw him again. There was never a funeral service, so I never knew if he was dead or alive. Their son's name was Jose and he never mentioned anything to me about his dad.

Chapter Six

One of my favorite activities, other than playing baseball or stickball, was going to school at PS 6. It provided an outlet for me to be away from home for a good part of the day. It was only a block away once we moved to Vyse Avenue, so it was easy to get to. I had to cross Tremont Avenue and it was right at the corner. I wanted to do well in school because I wanted to please my teachers, more so, believe it or not, than my parents. I was lucky to have teachers who truly cared about the kids they had the responsibility to teach. Over the years I have heard of numerous stories in the media chastising the New York City public school system as being overrun by mediocre teachers, but in twelve years going to public school, I can say without hesitation that I never encountered a mediocre or a bad teacher. All the teachers I was lucky to have were true educators and mentors for me. In many ways, school became a safe haven for me. And because I was fortunate to have good teachers, I looked forward to going to school every day.

Some teachers went out of their way to protect me whenever I got into trouble. During one special assembly, I was running around the auditorium instead of paying attention to the teacher's instructions because she wasn't my teacher. She became frustrated and grabbed me by one arm to scold me and get me in line. My teacher, Mrs. Israel, who I felt close to because of her name, saw that and reacted to protect me. She raised her voice at the other teacher and told her to never put her hands on one of her students. I was surprised that Mrs. Israel would come to my defense like that. Up until that point in my life, no one had interceded to protect me from any harm. Mrs. Israel was much older than the other teacher and seemed to command respect.

From that day on, Mrs. Israel was my favorite teacher at that school, and one who left a positive impression on me. She motivated me and inspired me to do well in school. I wanted Mrs. Israel to be proud of me. It was more important to me to please Mrs. Israel than to please my parents. They never looked at, or reviewed, my homework, so they never knew if I was doing well in school until I brought home a report card.

Sometimes I got lazy and skipped doing my homework. This was probably in protest because no one at home ever reviewed my work anyway. Perhaps it was a way of getting attention from my parents so they would get involved. I knew it would be reflected in my report card at some point. The problem was that when I brought home a bad report card, my parents just scolded me or cursed at me.

One of my favorite things at school was going on field trips. We were away from the school and classroom, traveling on a school bus and eating lunch somewhere other than the school cafeteria. One morning I was getting ready to go to school on a day we were scheduled to go on a field trip, and I went to the corner candy store to buy some candy to include in my lunch bag for the trip. The candy store had a double door that was made of a heavy metal frame and both doors swung open. The left door could be pushed open as someone was leaving the store, and the right one did the same as someone walked in.

Somehow, I opened the door with my hand too close to the edge. While I held one door to open it, the other door slammed my finger. It hurt so much that I didn't stay to buy my candy. I hurried home in pain. But I didn't want to complain and risk not going on the school trip, so I packed my lunch and headed to school.

I was in excruciating pain on the bus as my finger was throbbing, and I had to tell my teacher. My fingernail had turned purple and eventually fell off weeks later. But I was able to go on the school trip and was glad I did, even though the pain prevented me from doing much to have fun. I remember that I never allowed pain to stop me from doing something I wanted to do. I was growing up to be determined, persistent, and focused, if not incredibly obstinate.

One day when I was ten years old, I decided I wasn't going to school. My parents never knew that I didn't attend school that day. I wanted to experience what it was like to play hooky. There was a section of the Bronx River that a couple of friends and I went to, near 180th Street and Boston Road, and we were seeking adventure that sunny summer morning. The river around the area had a ledge that created a waterfall where the river dropped to a lower level. It was just a few blocks from home.

We each decided to cross to the other side of the river by walking across the top of the waterfall. We could have easily walked across either 180th Street or the edge of the park where there is an overpass to the river, but that wasn't the objective. It was to walk across the waterfall to prove that we could successfully get across the river. As we each walked gingerly across the ledge, with the water running over our feet, I slipped on the mossy metal base of the ledge and nearly fell below where the water splashed onto large rocks. I managed to catch my balance and prevent myself from falling. I was already almost halfway across, so turning back, which I thought about for an instant, didn't seem any safer. I was in no-man's land. Plus, my two friends had already made it across to the other side, so I wasn't about to be the one who didn't make it. I continued until I made it to the other side.

I always remember that adventure because it was rather scary as I stood up there over the middle of the Bronx River. Had I fallen I would have been *in* the river, and possibly badly injured on the rocks. This was another experience of mine that my parents never knew about.

The only thing that kept me from these types of potentially dangerous adventures, or trouble in general, was playing baseball. But my parents never enrolled me in things like Little League baseball or the YMCA to keep me off the streets. I was pretty much on my own.

Having to support a household of seven people on my dad's factory salary must have been a great challenge. My parents were never able to save any money for a rainy day. It might have been prudent, even on Dad's factory salary, for them to stash away a few bucks every week, but they didn't think that way. We were poor, so if my dad ever got sick, which he did a few times when I was young, Mom had to go on welfare to pay the rent and buy food for us.

We were still living on 179th Street when Dad had to stay in the hospital for an operation. He had developed a hernia and needed to have it repaired. He was unable to work for a week or so, and I guess he wasn't getting paid from Sunshine Biscuits.

When you live hand to mouth as we did, even one week without work means no food on the table. As kids, we didn't know what that meant, so we kept going about our days as usual. One afternoon one of my uncles stopped by with a box of groceries for us. It was David, the uncle who later got his nose bloodied by Dad. I was impressed that David had traveled on the subway carrying a box of food for us. It was a noble gesture on his part. I wondered why we needed to have someone other than Dad bring groceries to us, but Mom never explained that we were short on money for food. Just by observing and listening to her conversations, I could tell something was not right. She was grateful to David for his good deed and his concern for us.

One afternoon a few days later, I was in front of our building when I saw Dad walking toward me from the subway station. He had left the hospital early to get home to us. I thought that was pretty heroic of him. I didn't know how serious the hernia operation was, but I thought he was walking pretty fast for someone who was operated on just a couple of days prior. I thought that he was risking busting some stitches or something. Since he was a veteran of the Korean War, whenever he had to stay in the hospital, he went to the VA hospital in the Bronx. Over the years he had a number of hospital stays to treat ulcers. He never talked to us about his health, but he must have been stressed about not having enough money to cover the family's living expenses.

Along the way I was lucky to find someone who helped me get more involved playing baseball. Mom had a friend, Julia, who lived across the street from us, and she had a nephew who was an amateur baseball player. He liked teaching kids the game, and took me under his wing. We called him Papo and I never knew his real name, although I have an uncle whose name is Raphael and we call him Papo. Maybe Papo's real name was also Raphael.

Papo was much older than I was. When we first met I was maybe eight years old and he was probably sixteen. He often gathered a group of kids who were about the same age as I was, and organized baseball practices and pickup games. When we played games at the baseball field in West Farms Square, Papo pitched and the kids would alternate playing catcher. We could never get two full teams to play a real game, but we had enough kids to cover the infield, so we could hit and run the bases.

Papo had a car whose trunk he stuffed with all the baseball equipment we needed. He had gloves for all the kids, bats, balls, helmets, and a catcher's mask. I recall seeing the baseball duffel bag when he opened his trunk and being amazed at all the equipment. He even had bases.

Papo came by our apartment as early as 7 a.m. to pick me up and then gather the other kids to go to the baseball field. I was thrilled to be able to play on a real baseball field with grass, infield dirt, an outfield with nice grass, a warning track, and a fence to hit a homerun over. It was a joy to kick the dirt around home plate as I prepared myself to wait for one of Papo's pitches or slide into one of the bases. I fantasized about playing one day at Yankee Stadium.

Having Papo as my coach was the only way I could play baseball in a real baseball setting. In retrospect, it was perfect for my parents because it got me out of the house and away from windows I might break. At the same time it satisfied my desire to play the sport I came to love, but at no cost to them. It also did not require that they take me to the games. Mom trusted Papo and felt I was safe with him.

Papo was another mentor I was lucky to find early in my life. It was nice to have someone who cared about something I cared about like baseball, and I was blessed to have someone like him as a friend. He planted a valuable seed in me. The generosity with which he shared his time to teach me about the game, something Dad didn't have the time or the patience to do, showed me that it was possible to meet good people willing to do good deeds.

So I had Mrs. Israel at school as my teacher and mentor, who helped me remain focused on my educational performance, and Papo outside of school to help me stay out of trouble by playing baseball.

Most of us wore sneakers, but a few of the kids had metal cleats. I thought that was so cool and wanted a pair myself, but could never afford them until many years later.

During one game, I was playing third base. The player at the plate got a base hit into the outfield. There was a runner at first who rounded second and was on his way to third. I was covering the base well, and waiting for the throw. The throw and the runner got to me at about the same time. As the runner slid into the base, I was spiked on my index finger, which was sticking out of my glove. I remember yelling, "I got spiked, I got spiked!" My finger was bloody, and I jumped up and down. The opening on my finger was filled with dirt, so I could not see how serious it was, but I panicked and thought the worst—that I was going to have to go to the hospital and get stitches. I had never had stitches before and imagined that would hurt even more.

Papo walked over to see my injury when he saw and heard my dramatic reaction. He told me it wasn't bad at all. We went into the firehouse at the park and got it cleaned up. It just needed a bandage and there was no need to go to the hospital. I didn't play anymore that day and waited to go home, exhausted from screaming. My finger healed in a few days and I was able to go out and play ball again.

My friendship with Papo ended when we moved away from the Bronx in 1968. Sometime after we moved, Mom told me that Papo had died. I was very sad to hear that. He was a kind and giving person, and he taught me a great deal about baseball and friendship. A combination of time, a common interest like baseball, and encouragement helped me escape from the chaos I encountered at home.

He taught me that you can make a positive impact on a young person's life by just giving a little of your time.

Chapter Seven

I could never understand why my parents' reaction to everything that did not please them was with physical or verbal violence. The verbal violence was usually hurtful words like *stupid*, *idiot*, or Spanish curse words that Dad called me when he got upset. He was usually more verbal than physical with his abusive behavior, although he was the one who would slap me on the head or poke me with a stick to extricate me from under the bed where I hid to avoid a beating.

When I was eight, nine, or ten years old, I didn't understand what the word meant, but when Dad got angry with me, he sometimes called me *maricon*. The word in Spanish means "faggot." That he called me that shocked me years later when I learned what it meant. He continued to call me that through my teenage years whenever he got mad, which was often. My resentment of him grew deeper as he continually directed profanities at me in Spanish for the simplest offenses. If I walked in front of the television and blocked his view, I would hear *hijodelagranputa*, son of a grand whore. If I dropped something, I would be called *pendejo*, idiot. Even when I didn't know what the words meant, his condescending tone told me he wasn't calling me a nice name.

He also tried to continue to beat me with a belt or slap me around, but as I got older I think he actually began to be afraid of me. Once I started retaliating against his attempts to beat me at about fourteen years old, he didn't hit me anymore. He and Mom taught me how to be physically and verbally violent. What they didn't count on was that it was only a matter of time before I projected onto them what I had been taught.

Mom also used words to instill guilt as a way to get me to be obedient or give her something she wanted.

One Halloween I was out trick-or-treating in the neighborhood. In the Bronx in the 1960s, Halloween was a very lucrative holiday for kids like me. Most of the residents gave coins instead of candy. Some gave both. An eight- or nine-year-old kid like me could make five, maybe six dollars, plus candy.

I never had a costume, so I usually painted my face with Halloween paint I bought at the candy store on the corner of Tremont and Vyse Avenues. If I didn't have money to buy the paint, I trick-or-treated long enough to accumulate the money. That one year I started trick-or-treating in the afternoon, visiting all the apartment buildings in the neighborhood. It was also customary to trick-or-treat on the street as we saw people walking in the neighborhood. The neighbors were always quite nice and generous.

Since we lived only a block or two from the subway station where the IRT number 5 train stopped at the Tremont Avenue station, I thought it would be lucrative to trick-or-treat at the station. I had seen a commercial on television where kids were trick-or-treating for UNICEF. I had no idea what that was, but it seemed that kids were making good money this way. I went alone down to the train station at five in the afternoon and stood at the foot of the stairs and asked for treats as people came home from work. I held my hand out as I repeated, "Trick-or-treat for UNICEF." It was amazing that people would give me quarters as a treat. I was so busy that by about eight that evening, I had to go home to unload all my winnings of the day.

There was one building across the street from our apartment that I had not visited yet, so I asked Mom to let me go to that last building to complete my Halloween. She didn't want me to go, but I begged and she acquiesced. I entered the lobby of the building and noticed that it was quite active and noisy, with kids trick-or-treating and neighbors with their doors open, handing out candy and money.

I went up to the second floor and knocked on a door. It had closed after some kids finished visiting just a minute before, so I knew the people were at home. When the lady opened the door, I saw a small dog running out toward me. I got scared and ran up the stairs to get away, but the dog followed me. It was a Jack Russell terrier and it jumped up at me and bit me just below my belly button. I was scared and started crying, and ran out of the building and across the street to our home.

Mom's response to me, after looking at the bite mark, was that this happened because I went across the street against her wishes. She didn't take me to the hospital for a tetanus shot, and she didn't console me. I thought she could have gotten her message across differently and weaved it in as she consoled me, but I guess she didn't know how to do that. It was relayed as another punishment from God. Somehow, God was always the culprit in doling out punishment. Years later she wondered and chastised me for my lack of faith in God. How could I have faith in a God who, according to her, was constantly punishing me? She made it so I wanted to stay as far away from him as possible. It seemed that everyone else he forgave, but me he punished.

God was the ultimate authority figure. Below him were Mom and Dad. I could not trust or count on them, so how could I trust God? Two things happened on my way to church. First, I ascribed to God the mistrustful attributes that I envisioned in my parents; and second, Mom, by constantly attributing my punishment to God, drove me away from him. It wasn't her intention, but it is what happened. Healthy faith in God is a mighty powerful thing. It helps you believe that anything is possible. After all, faith is belief. It is said that you have to believe before you can see. I was driven to have to see before I could believe. That was an impossible task where religion is concerned.

I've often wondered what kind of childhood my parents each had that made them the way they were. Mom was one of eleven surviving children (my grandparents had fifteen children, but four died as infants). Most were born in Puerto Rico, except for the two youngest, Ivan and Millie. They were born in New York City after my grandparents emigrated from the island in 1946. My grandmother, Domitila, was always quite grumpy. Some people reason that, having given birth to fifteen children, she had earned the privilege to be grumpy. My grandfather, Julio, on the other hand was very nice, warm, and caring.

Grandma Domitila died about twenty-five years ago, when she was in her mid-seventies. She was always scolding me to eat my food, not walk too hard on her floors, and sit still. It seemed that she scolded me every time I saw her. To me she was not a very likable lady. Come to think of it, the only time she didn't scold me was when she wanted a favor from me. Sometimes she took advantage of my arrival at their house to have me go to the grocery store for her, even though my uncles and aunts were at the house and any one of them could have gone.

Grandma was especially protective of her children. She seemed to have difficulty letting go of them as they grew up and developed relationships with boyfriends and girlfriends. To protect them from potentially undesirable relationships, occasionally she used me as her spy.

My uncle Robert began dating a woman from Central America who lived in the neighborhood, and Grandma was suspicious of her—jealous that she might lose her son to the new girlfriend. One afternoon she stopped me outside her home as I walked by 94th Street. She had noticed the woman was walking up the road on her way toward Junction Boulevard. With the promise of twenty-five cents, she asked me to follow the woman to see where she was going and report back to her. I did as she asked me, but found nothing devious to report.

Nevertheless, I enjoyed going to my grandparents' house, but only because I wanted to see my grandfather and my uncles and aunts. Most of them were young enough that I could do things with them, but old enough that they could mentor me and teach me new things. All the time that I was at their house, I never saw my grandmother being mean or physically violent to any of my ten aunts and uncles.

Grandpa Julio was always pleasant and nice to me. He was actually nicer to me than my dad. Every time I saw him, he would kiss me on the cheek and say, "*Que Dios te bendiga,*" which in Spanish means "May God bless you."

I did realize that he had a bad temper if he got upset. Mom must have certainly inherited his genes, because she could be sweet but turn violent in an instant. There was only one occasion when I witnessed him being physical with any of his children.

We lived in Queens when I was about twelve years old, and I was playing around with my uncle Ivan, who was four years older than me. Ivan was very athletic and strong. He was into martial arts, track and field, and weight training. I idolized him because he was very cool and close in age to me. As the years passed, the four-year difference became less and less significant, and we grew closer. We actually went to high school together. He was a senior when I was a freshman. He was a track star in high school and popular among school athletes and teachers.

I joined the Newtown High School track team just to be closer with Ivan. He mentored me as we trained together. As part of our training we typically jogged home after having practiced at the school track field. The distance from there to home was about two miles. Ivan encouraged me to train hard and I didn't want to let him down.

One day, we were in front of my grandparents' house and Ivan grabbed me by the arm and twisted it. He was playing, but it hurt. Grandpa was coming home from work and saw what Ivan had done to me. He grabbed Ivan, scolded him, and told him never to hit me again. It wasn't a violent reaction, but it was definitely a firm one. Ivan did not protest and I could tell that he respected Grandpa.

Although I didn't really like being with my grandmother, I occasionally spent the night in their house. It was a big single-family house on Hoe Avenue in the South Bronx, so it was a treat for me compared to the cramped apartment we lived in. There was always lots of action outside the house, with kids playing stickball, riding scooters made from wooden milk cartons, boards, and skates. The kids with the scooters raced them up and down the street.

I looked up to my teenage aunts and uncles and felt closest to Ivan and Mike and Juanita (Nani) and Socorro (Cookie). Ivan and Mike were active in sports, especially baseball, so we had that in common, although I was still too young to play at their level. It was nice to be around them to see them play.

One summer morning I woke up as I always did, around 7 a.m. One thing I didn't like about Grandma's house was that they all slept pretty late in the morning. I wanted to go outside and play, but was afraid she might scold me if I made noise and woke her up, and I didn't want that. So I decided to try to get everyone to wake up so

I could play with Ivan. Someone had taught me a trick where you dialed a certain phone number, hung up, and the phone would ring back. It was a ring-back number the phone company used to test if your phone was working properly. I think the number was 555-1212, but I'm not sure as these ring-back numbers no longer exist. Kids would use it to fool parents into thinking there was a real call coming in. When the parents picked up the phone, all they heard was a dial tone.

I did this that one early morning and ran, softly so Grandma, who was in another room, wouldn't hear me, but fast enough so she wouldn't see me when she walked by to answer the phone. I got back in bed and pretended to be sleeping. She got up from her bed and went to the phone. Once she picked it up and heard only a dial tone, she cursed in Spanish and wondered out loud, *"Carajo, quien esta llamando a esta hora?"* "Who the hell is calling at this time?" When she went back to bed, I did it again. Again she got up, this time cursing in Spanish as she walked to pick up the phone. She was quite upset the second time when there was only a dial tone. I was quite amused by this little trick, but disappointed that it did not have the result I was seeking. Nobody got up so that I could go outside to play. I had to wait patiently for someone to get up so we could have breakfast and then go outside.

By 1967-68, my uncle Mike, who was six years older than me, was becoming a hippie and was very much into The Beatles' music. One day, when I was eleven years old, I was sitting around our apartment with nothing to do. Mom was taking a nap when Mike called the house and asked if I wanted to go with him to Times Square to see a movie. I woke up Mom and asked for permission, and she said it was okay. I had to meet Mike at my grandparents' house, so I hopped on the number 5 train at the Tremont Avenue station and rode the two stops to the Freeman Street station. By that time I was both familiar and comfortable with riding the subway alone and didn't hesitate to meet Mike at his house.

We went into Manhattan to see *Yellow Submarine*. It was the first time I had ever been to Times Square. I was amazed at all the lights and the activity. I was afraid of getting lost out there, so I stayed close to Mike. I didn't understand the movie, but because it was animated, I paid attention and tried to follow along. After the movie, Mike and I went into some of the stores in Times Square so he could buy posters to hang on the walls in his room at home.

That same summer of 1968, the entire extended family, little by little, made an exodus from the South Bronx to Queens. I remember that my oldest uncle, Carmelo, whom we have always called Lito, was the first to move to Queens with his wife and kids. I figured out that his nickname had evolved from Carmelito, or little Carmelo, to just Lito as he got older. The unwritten rule in the family was to give everyone a nickname of no more than two syllables so we did not have to repeat long names. Domitila was Tila; Socorro was Choco; Evelyn was Tata; Wilfredo was Chubby; Israel was Fatty, and so on. Lito had a second-story storefront apartment in Jackson Heights on 31st Avenue off 92nd Street.

My grandparents were the next to move there, into a two-family house on 92nd Street around the corner from Lito's apartment. They occupied the second floor of the house. A Haitian family lived on the first floor. It was a nicely sized apartment, and included a room in the attic that became Mike's hippie retreat. I liked going into that room because Mike had it set up with black lights, purple walls, lots of Beatles' posters, and he always had music playing.

One thing that struck me back then is that while my parents always lived in apartment buildings, my grandparents preferred to live in a one- or two-family house. They had more space than we had, as well as more privacy from neighbors.

My grandmother wanted Mom to move out there as well, so she had Lito find us an apartment nearby. I'm not certain if Dad or Mom ever went out there to see the apartment before actually renting it. It turns out that the Sunshine Biscuits factory, where my dad worked, was in Long Island City, so living in Jackson Heights or anywhere near there made his train commute much easier and shorter.

Chapter Eight

On the evening of June 28, 1968, we moved from the South Bronx to East Elmhurst. Our apartment was a two-bedroom, one-bath home above a candy store on Astoria Boulevard and the corner of 94th Street. The building was a pre-war multi-family structure with two apartments built in 1926, and our apartment was all of 852 square feet. It was attached to another apartment building that we shared an atrium with. We could walk onto the atrium from our kitchen and get to the other apartment through their kitchen window.

I remember riding in the moving truck with Lito. He was a bodybuilder who had amassed a number of trophies for events he won and did moving jobs on the side from his regular job, which was delivering furniture for the Bloomingdale's department store. He was amazing the way he was able to put a refrigerator on his back and walk it up the stairs to our apartment. Whenever anyone in the family moved to a new apartment, it was Lito who they hired to help them move. He kept his Bloomingdale's truck at home, so he was able to use it on the weekends and days off and make extra money.

We finished organizing the major things like the beds and dressers late that night, and left the rest of the unpacking for the next day. I was pretty tired and fell asleep on the couch in the living room. We never had air-conditioning in any of the apartments that we lived in, so we simply tolerated the heat. When I woke up the next morning, I was

sweaty and had black dirt on my neck. The apartment
was dusty and still needed a good cleaning.

That next morning I also woke up to my twelfth birthday. I didn't expect, and didn't have, any kind of
celebration, especially with the hectic time that the move
brought. Lito's oldest son, also named Israel but whom we
called Chiqui, came by the apartment early in the morning
with a couple of friends to look for me. I thought it was
really cool that in a new neighborhood I was able to
connect with cousins and their friends so quickly. We had
not been in the new neighborhood one full day yet, and I
already had friends to hang out with.

Chiqui was my age and had an interest in the same
sports as I did. Over the years we played baseball, basketball, touch football, and stickball together. That first
morning that he and the other guys came by for me, we just
walked around and they introduced me to the new neighborhood. As we walked down Astoria Boulevard, I felt like
I usually felt when I walked into a candy store. I was
amazed by the openness of the streets, which, like Astoria
Boulevard, we could walk on and not be bombarded by
large numbers of either people or cars. At the same time I
felt a sense of fresh air along the many tree-lined streets,
with rows and rows of single-family homes as opposed to
rows and rows of apartment buildings that were all too
common to me in the Bronx.

I didn't mention to Chiqui and the other kids that it
was my birthday. That one went by at home just like all the
previous ones. There was no cake or card. One would think
it would condition me to believe that birthdays were not
important and need not be celebrated. The opposite was
true though. As I got older, I always believed that someone's birthday—whether a brother, sister, relative, friend, or
coworker—was important and deserved to be celebrated. It

is only one day a year that we get to show someone how important they are.

The apartment next door to ours became vacant, and as the family migration from the South Bronx to Queens was being completed, my aunt Irma and her husband, Aladino, moved quickly to occupy it. Sometimes it's best not to have family living too close to you, though. Irma and Aladino's relationship was marred by frequent violence, and we had an up-close view of it. It's amazing that for all we hear through the news media, both in print and television, about domestic violence, there are many more cases of this type of abuse that tragically go unnoticed and unreported.

In the case of Irma and Aladino, what ignited Aladino's rage against his wife was always his drinking. He was a rather nasty drunk—a classic case of Dr. Jekyll and Mr. Hyde. When Aladino was sober he was pleasant and extremely generous. Unfortunately, he had an affinity for beer and would drink lots of it, almost nightly after he returned home from work and definitely on the weekends. Through our apartment walls we always knew when he was drunk. That is when we heard Irma's screams and cries for help as Aladino beat her. Mom and Dad were too pusillanimous to interfere, so they just let it happen. On numerous occasions I prodded them to go over to the apartment to at least interrupt the fracas. I thought that if Mom or Dad knocked on their door under the pretense of visiting, it might extinguish Aladino's fiery rage. They had two little girls, Fofi and Sylvia, as well, who had to be witnesses to the routine violence.

We often hear how a victim of domestic abuse, usually the wife, is reluctant to press criminal charges against her husband, preferring to believe that the last time it occurred was truly the last time. It was no different with Irma and Aladino. Mom finally confronted her sister on another calm occasion and asked her if she wanted help to deal with the abuse she was clearly being subjected to. Irma refused any help, expressing confidence that she and Aladino could handle their own differences privately.

The owners of the building where we lived, Fred and Nellie, also operated the candy store below us. One day Aladino went into the store and got into a fight with the husband and wife team. It might have been over late payment of the rent.

There was another person, a friend of Fred and Nellie's, there at the time. He must have said something to Aladino that he didn't like, and Aladino felt compelled to engage the man in a fight. As the two of them struggled, Aladino pulled out a knife and stabbed the man in the stomach. I was upstairs, along with Mom and other siblings, when we heard what had happened. The police arrived and the place was like a scene you might see on the evening news.

Aladino left the area quickly before the police arrived. The police officers were asking where they could find him, and the ambulance took the stabbing victim away. Luckily, the man survived. My uncle Ivan came by from Grandma's house, a few blocks away, to find out what had happened. Mom was outside and, seeing the police place Ivan in the backseat of their car, became hysterical. She assumed that Ivan was being arrested and began screaming at the police, pleading with them to let Ivan go.

It turned out that Ivan told them he knew where Aladino was hiding. Ivan was not a suspect and was not handcuffed, but Mom didn't notice that and just went berserk with the police. One of the officers tried to calm her down by telling her that Ivan was not arrested, that he was just trying to help them. He said, "See, he's not even handcuffed."

They drove to Grandma's home and found Aladino crouched behind a chair in the living room. I don't know what the outcome was because no one in the family openly talked about it, at least not around me. All I knew was that Aladino was arrested, but he did not spend much time in jail. He was home within days. I guess he was lucky that the person he stabbed survived.

That episode was the second time in my young life that I experienced a relative being arrested. The other time was a few years prior to the Aladino arrest. We were still living in the South Bronx when Irma and Juanita knocked on our door late one evening. Mom let them in and was informed that William, another uncle, had been arrested that evening. William was a teenager at the time and had been hanging out with the wrong crowd when they broke into a closed store and were caught by the police.

In both cases, William and Aladino were released from custody without having to serve a jail term.

Chapter Nine

When we first moved to Queens, I thought it was like being in the country. We were surrounded by trees on every street. There was less congestion of cars and people. There were fewer large apartment buildings and projects too, at least in the area of East Elmhurst and Jackson Heights where our family lived.

By the time I was twelve years old, we had lived in five different apartments. Stability of any kind was not an element that we were accustomed to at home. It always felt to me like we were running away from something. But for some reason I was looking forward to the move to Queens.

I actually liked the change I found in East Elmhurst, especially because we were much closer to cousins and the entire family of uncles and aunts. I didn't have to get on the subway to go see them. Everyone was within a few blocks from our apartment. After the summer, Mom enrolled me at PS 127 in East Elmhurst to start the new school year in the sixth grade.

I remember the first day of school. I always sat at the front of the classroom because I wanted to be close to the teacher. That way I could be called upon to answer questions or write on the board. I even enjoyed being assigned board-washing duty. I was a kid looking for the recognition that I did not get at home.

I can only imagine how much farther I might have gone in school if Mom and Dad had encouraged me and supported my interest in learning. As a young student I needed, as all kids do, guidance and leadership from my

parents to help me open more doors in my own education. I could have done much more than simply go to class
and do my homework. Unfortunately, Mom and Dad did
not grow up themselves with encouragement from their
parents to attend school, and education was not important
to them. Whatever success I was going to enjoy in school
would be as a result of mentors and supporters I was lucky
to meet in school itself or in the neighborhoods we lived in.
That, coupled with my own innate drive and aspirations,
propelled my education.

PS 127 School where I attended my first year in Queens,
sixth grade.

Anyway, on my first day of school, I sat in the front of
the classroom. To my left was a kid named Devan. The
physical and verbal abuse I experienced at home made me
an angry kid outside with other kids. I felt a need to hit
someone, and it didn't take much for me to get into a fight.
When I was at PS 6 in the Bronx, I got into fights at school
occasionally, but by the time I was twelve and nearing my

teenage years, I was becoming angrier and lashing out more frequently.

The kids at school tended to sit close to one another as they shared space on long tables. That day, Devan's leg touched mine. In retrospect, I don't think he did it purposely, but I jumped out of my seat and punched him in the chest. I really don't know to this day what came over me, but it was an instinct to protect myself that made me react and lash out that way. At that time in my life, it was safer to retaliate for being touched outside of my home than to do so against either of my parents at home. For the time being!

Devan did not react at that moment. During our lunch break we were outside and we fought on the sidewalk. Devan was a quiet kid, but he became my number one nemesis all through high school. After that one year at PS 127, we both attended Intermediate School 145 in Jackson Heights. We never fought at that school. After two years there, where we attended seventh and eighth grade, we both moved on to Newtown High School in Elmhurst. We used to take a public bus to school and on occasion we became entangled and fought on the bus. During one fight, I had him in a bear hug while he punched my face. I pushed him against the large window at the back of the bus, it popped open, and I nearly pushed him out. That's when we decided to stop fighting. We both came away from that fight with bruises as our supposed friends on the bus looked on and cheered the battle. The bus driver did nothing to stop it.

A few years after high school, I learned from a mutual friend, a guy we called Jelly because he was fat and jiggled when he walked, that Devan had killed his father. Jelly told me that Devan waited behind a door at their home and when his dad entered the house, Devan slashed his throat.

Apparently, his sister was killed in a car accident and Devan blamed his father.

The years when I was eleven, twelve, and thirteen were important ones for me as I tried to distance myself more and more from my parents. I was learning to fend for myself in many ways, but still had to deal with their negative and violent behavior toward my siblings and me.

My brother Wil was ten years old when he and Susan, who was eight, were fighting over a toy in the living room. Susan began crying and, as kids tend to do, went to Mom for help in retrieving her toy. The fact that she was crying and screaming enraged Mom. She marched into the living room where Wil was sitting and punched him in the face, bloodying his nose. Hearing the loud commotion, I hurried out of our bedroom, where I was looking out the window. Immediately, my instinct was to get a towel and clean up Wil's face. Mom never apologized, and Wil never forgot.

With behavior like that being an integral part of our unfortunate upbringing, how could we not be violent kids when we were outside?

I have to say that most of the lessons I learned at home were teaching me what not to do. I knew that I did not want to emulate my parents. The way they treated us didn't seem right to me. It seemed that everything they did was based on selfishness and with no regard for setting a good example for their kids.

I still went to the supermarket with Dad on 37th Avenue and Junction Boulevard each Thursday, but did all I could to limit my interaction with him and Mom. He and I always walked there from Astoria Boulevard, and that was maybe seven or eight blocks from home. Dad and I no longer went to ballgames together.

There is a lesson to be imparted in everything we do, but my parents were oblivious to that notion. Dad did not think that all of the things he did around me were learning experiences for me. Once the lesson was absorbed, I had to decide to either emulate or detest the behavior. With each lesson that my parents taught me, my level of respect for them diminished.

At the supermarket my dad wanted to get as much value for his money as possible, but he never used coupons. Instead, he would lean over the meat shelves, pull off the price ticket from a lower priced pack of meat, and casually place it over a more expensive pack. That is how he got more meat for his money to feed a family of seven. I saw him doing this every week that we went to the supermarket. He was never caught, so it was easy not to stop.

It never occurred to him that I was there and this was the example he was setting for me. That didn't matter to him. He was always trying to get something for free. I wonder what he would have done if he got caught switching the prices on items. Would the supermarket manager call the police and have him arrested? I was afraid that he would get caught and we would both get in trouble. He never explained to me why he did it and he never advised me not to follow his example. He acted as though he was proud that he got away with it.

I don't think he ever believed in "do as I say, not as I do." It was examples like that which taught me that it was okay to steal, as long as you did not get caught. It was a mentality of getting away with whatever you could to get something for nothing. I wish that he would have worked harder; perhaps worked overtime to earn more money. It would have been much more positive, of course, for him to show us kids the value of aspiration, hard work, striving to be better, pride, and love. Unfortunately, that was not his style.

Mom didn't mind much either when I told her what he had done repeatedly at the supermarket.

By the time I was thirteen years old, I stopped going to the supermarket with Dad. I believe that each of us reaches a fork in the road, and I could have followed the path that was paved with all the experiences I accumulated at home, or I could have followed the road that was paved with my innate direction, the instincts that somehow formed my wishes and desires. Deep down I felt that it was my destiny to rise above all that I had seen and was exposed to. I can't explain it, other than to say that my calling was different; I had to chart my own path.

In my case, I knew at an early age that I was different. I somehow knew that despite all the beatings, all the violence I had witnessed, all the humiliating words shouted at me, I was not like my parents. That does not mean all of those negative experiences did not have an influence on me. They did indeed. They were experiences that shaped how I would behave with others for years. But they also fostered an appreciation for opposing characteristics—kindness, generosity, and understanding, being industrious, calm.

The challenge was how long it would take for me to reverse the effects of those experiences and become a better person—not one in the image of my parents. That proved to be a huge, lifelong challenge.

It amounted to a lifestyle change focused on reflection about who I was becoming as a human being. I had to contemplate if I wanted to be surrounded by positive individuals who were grateful, supportive of others, and independent thinkers; or those who were immersed in a life led by complaining, criticizing others, and co-dependency. I didn't care for the latter!

Chapter Ten

At the age of twelve, tired of asking for a quarter, only to be rejected and ridiculed, I talked my way into a job at the neighborhood deli, which was located just downstairs from our apartment, and next door to Fred and Nellie's candy store.

Nelson had worked in the bodega in the Bronx when he was ten or eleven years old, so I thought I could work at twelve. I had no idea that there was a minimum age or that I would need working papers at some age. I don't think my parents knew about those rules either.

The owner of the deli was Russell Lucas. He was a very nice man and took a liking to me, so he gave me a job stocking the shelves and refrigerators and sweeping the floors. I started out working two hours a day, for which Russell paid me one dollar for each hour.

Soon after that, Russell had me working behind the counter with him, helping to fill customer orders. Russell taught me how to work the cash register and make change for customers. I enjoyed working there, and was proud of the fact that I could work and earn my own money. Eventually, Russell allowed me to make sandwiches and take care of customers all by myself. I was proud of the fact that he trusted me.

Russell gave me a metal vase in his office in the back of the store where I was able to safely save my money. Each time I got paid I stashed the money in that vase. I used to set savings targets for myself to have something to strive for. This was something that I learned by myself, with Russell's guidance. I was also motivated by seeing that my parents never had extra money. It didn't feel like a secure way of living.

By that time, I became the first and only saver in the family. If I made ten dollars per week, by the end of the month I had forty dollars. That was suddenly a huge sum for me at twelve years of age. Sneakers back then cost around ten dollars, so to have enough to buy four pairs was exciting.

The experience working for Russell was an important one in developing my own identity. Suddenly, I had less time to go to the supermarket with Dad. After school I hurried home, changed my clothes to be more comfortable, and ran downstairs to work at the deli.

During the week I was soon working four hours per day and I would also work on weekends, usually in the evenings. Russell had a small television behind the counter so he and I could watch baseball games, or the Knicks, while we worked. He was a big Mets and Knicks fan. I was pleased to know that I could leave my earnings in the back of the store in the vase that Russell lent me, and not worry that it might be stolen.

By working for Russell I learned that I could trust someone. In all the time that I worked for him and saved my money in the store, I never lost any of it. He even had other people working at the store, and no one ever bothered with the vase. Three women worked at the store at different times so he could attend to store business, such as paperwork in the office in the back of the store, or go to the Hunts Point market in the Bronx to replenish some food supplies. Other items like ice cream and chips were delivered to the store.

Occasionally, he invited me to go with him to the market. Those were exciting trips because I got to see a different aspect of how the deli operated, and I got to ride in his sports car, a 1969 Camaro. Russell was a great mentor for me and an inspiration in my wanting to do well in school. I wanted to show him that I was smart and interested in doing well.

Sometimes when the deli was slow, he and I went outside just in front of the store and played catch. If a customer walked into the store, we stopped playing and Russell followed behind to attend to their needs.

Mom and Dad were happy that I had a job when I was twelve. They benefitted in multiple ways. One way in which they benefitted was that I started buying my own clothes. Once I had enough money saved up and had reached a target I had set for myself, I went out to buy my Converse Chuck Taylor sneakers or a pair of jeans.

Usually, I bought my sneakers at the Army and Navy store on Junction Boulevard near Roosevelt Avenue. That was the same store where Ivan swiped items from time to time. He didn't work because all of his free time was devoted to track and field at Newtown. If he needed a new pair of shorts, something easy to hide, he and I walked into the Army and Navy store. He went into the dressing room with two pairs and asked me to look out and let him know if anyone was coming to the back of the store where the dressing room was.

He never tried on either pair. He knew what size he needed. Instead, he stuffed one in the front of his pants, and then returned the other to the shelf. The store clerk or owner saw him returning a pair of shorts to the shelf and assumed it didn't fit. Ivan and I casually walked out of the store.

I never had the nerve to do something like that. I always paid for the things I wanted. If I didn't have enough money for something, I saved until I had enough.

Once I got used to having money saved, it became a habit. The more I saved, the more I wanted to save. What a concept! It demonstrated to me that it was possible to have money and see the pile grow.

When I saw that my savings in Russell's vase had grown to fifty dollars, I set a new savings target for myself. I wanted to know what it felt like to have one hundred dollars. I had not seen a one-hundred-dollar bill before that time, and thought it would be fun to be able to exchange a hundred dollars in savings for one of those bills.

At thirteen years of age, I had become more aware of my appearance, especially with girls. I wanted to dress nicely and I saved enough money to buy myself a black leather jacket.

Whenever I met a savings target for the purpose of buying clothes, I took the subway to Delancey Street in lower Manhattan, where I could buy clothing that I liked at good prices. Sometimes I traveled there with Mom and sometimes alone or with a friend. On one visit I noticed that they had some beautiful and colorful sweaters for the upcoming fall and winter season. I decided to save enough money to buy some to add to my wardrobe collection. I bought a brown knitted sweater with white and tan leather patches on the front and a light blue one with red and yellow designs on the sleeves and the collar. I also bought some dress pants with flaps on the back pockets to coordinate with the sweaters. They were all hip 1970s designs.

All the other kids at IS 145 looked up to me because I always had great clothes and shoes. Most of my friends were Puerto Rican and black, and the clothing we wore was very different from what the white kids wore. But while most kids went to school with the same clothes and sneakers every day, I frequently wore a different outfit. I wore Playboy shoes, which were popular in the 1960s and '70s, silk pants with flaps over the back pockets, and colorful sweaters in the winter, or colorful polo shirts or silk T-shirts in the summer. Even my Chuck Taylors looked

stylish with the contrasting color laces I added to them—
red laces for my white pair, and purple laces for my black
pair. I was quickly becoming more independent, even in
how I dressed. Still, I was impatient and wanted to move
faster.

I regularly gave Mom half the money I earned at the
deli. If I made four dollars I would give her two and save
two in Russell's vase. If by the end of the week I had
accumulated twenty dollars in earnings, I gave half to Mom.
Suddenly, she was nice to me because I was giving her
money. Dad was happy because I no longer asked him for
money. A problem arose when I made the mistake of
telling them that I had saved my share of the earnings and
was going shopping for a new pair of Chuck Taylors. I had
twenty dollars and Mom asked me to give her ten. I could
not understand why she wanted to have half of what I
saved for myself. Her request, or demand, seemed unfair to
me. The problem I saw with her logic was that my twenty
dollars was the half I had saved after having given half to
her previously. It was classic double taxation!

Mom must have thought we had some contract that
stipulated that whatever money I had at any time was 50
percent hers. I protested and told her that I had already
given her half of what I had earned and this was my half,
which I had saved so I could buy some clothes. She became furious, and yelled and screamed. Eventually, she
frightened me into giving her the ten dollars. After I
handed her the ten-dollar bill, I became furious and sad at
the same time when her next reaction was to indignantly
say she did not need my money, and she ripped the ten-
dollar bill into too many pieces for me to paste back
together. I couldn't believe she would do that just to hurt
me.

She was a grown woman of thirty-three—a mom
fighting with a thirteen-year-old over ten dollars. It was yet

another example of the selfishness and greed that prevailed in everything she and Dad did. He sat there in the
living room, but said nothing. As far as they were both
concerned, it was my fault. It wasn't long before I heard
that God had punished me for being greedy.

By example Mom demonstrated how she cared only
about herself and what she could get from me. She and
Dad were takers and not givers. It had nothing to do with
teaching me about money management or fairness. It was
much to the contrary. She had already spent the half of my
earnings which I had given her, and upon learning I had
saved my half, she felt she should get half of that as well
simply because she was my mom.

The lesson I got out of that experience was that I
could not tell anyone in our home how much money I had
at any time. If I told my siblings, they would tell Mom and
she would demand that I give her some. If I told Mom, she
would try to take it from me. It was truly a sad situation
because I was conditioned into being overly self-protective
and detached from them.

Despite that, I was happy working because it gave me
a level of independence that enabled me to do things I
otherwise could not do. I started to venture out, looking
for other means of earning money. On Saturday mornings,
I walked to the supermarket on 99th Street and Astoria
Boulevard to bag groceries and help customers take their
groceries to their cars for tips. I don't know why Dad never
went to that supermarket for our groceries since it was a
few blocks closer than the Foodtown on Junction Boulevard.

Bagging groceries for a few hours in the morning each
Saturday made me another couple of bucks in tips. I
alternated between that supermarket and the Dan's Supreme located on Northern Boulevard and 90th Street,
across the street from the locally famous Sam's Pizzeria. It

was liberating to be able to buy my own clothes, have control over how I dressed, go to the movies when I wanted, and buy my school supplies when I needed. Most importantly, I did all that while no longer having to ask my parents for money.

With a White Castle across the street from Dan's Supreme, whatever change I made bagging groceries usually got deposited right in the neighborhood in exchange for a few burgers, fries, and a Coke or chocolate shake. Throughout my teenage years the White Castle and Sam's Pizzeria were favorite hangouts for my friends and me.

The most important thing I did was learn to save money. I felt almost a peaceful and relaxed sensation that came from working hard and having something to show for it.

At the age of thirteen, I talked my way into another job at the local movie theatre. The Fair Theatre was about four blocks from home, right on Astoria Boulevard. My job was fairly easy. The manager wanted me to change the letters on the marquee one evening a week. On Thursdays I would remove that week's movies and put up the next week's showings. I had to climb up on a ladder and change the letters in about fifteen or twenty minutes. For that, he paid me two dollars and gave me two free movie passes. Plus, I could stay around the theatre that evening and view whatever was playing that night.

The manager required that the marquee be changed at night, so I would do that around 9 p.m. I thought this was a cool job because it made me feel as though I was on the inside as a member of the staff of the theatre, rather than a customer. It was fun to walk into the theatre without having to pay. Having the two free movie passes each week meant I could save more of the money I made at the deli and supermarkets, and still go to the movies. It was cool to see movies like *Beneath the Planet of the Apes* and *The Great White Hope* for free.

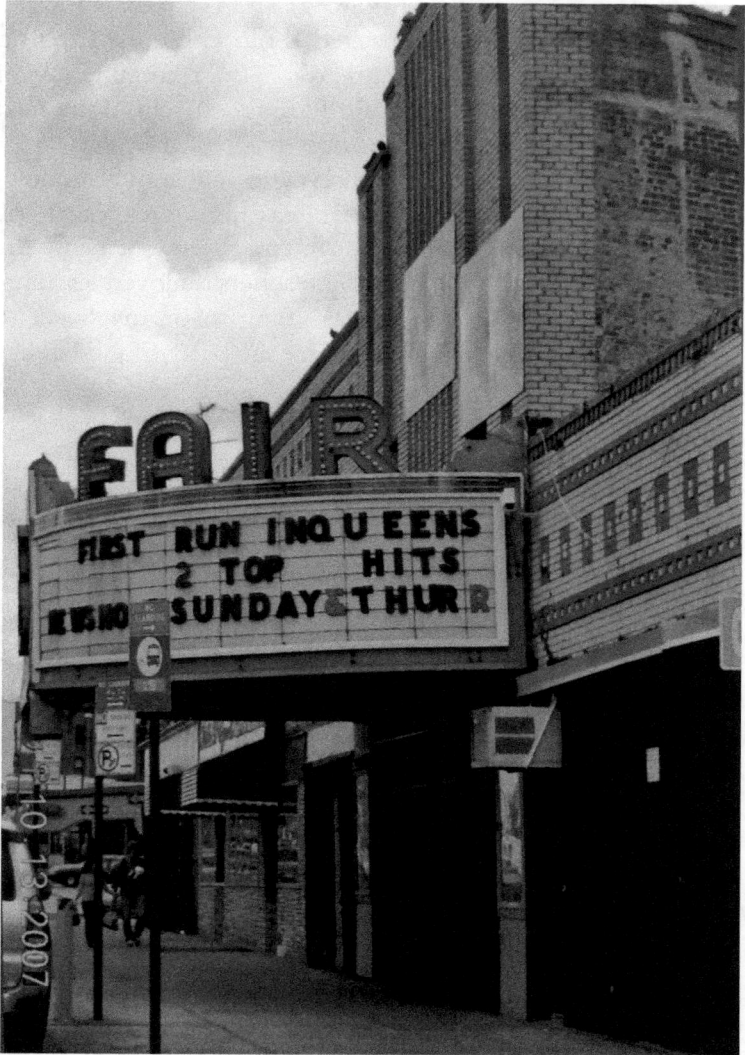

The Fair movie theatre on Astoria Boulevard where I worked changing the marquee lettering. Looks like they still have kids changing the letters.

Having these jobs instilled in me the confidence that I could do anything as long as I was willing to work hard. I was able to manage my schoolwork and the jobs without a problem. My parents never asked about either, so I felt no pressure to get my homework done by a certain time. I knew I could get it done before I arrived at school the next day or whenever the work was due.

I pretty much had to learn how to juggle my time myself. I made sure my schoolwork was done on time. I still liked school, so it wasn't a problem for me to find the motivation to do well. I liked my teachers, enjoyed learning, and believed that education was going to be my ticket to get out of my home and from under my parents' guidance.

Chapter Eleven

Between school and work I felt I had the two keys to one day escape from my unhappy home environment. I felt alone at home and didn't enjoy being there. Motivated by the prospect of one day getting out of there, I focused my energies on working harder at both earning money and learning in school. Soon I was scouting the streets on a mission to find more jobs where I could make and save more money.

As I spent more and more time outside of home, either working at the deli or the theatre, playing softball or basketball at the park, there was less opportunity for violence at home. I made sure of that by staying out as late as possible and only coming home to sleep. The apartment was infested with roaches and mice, so I absolutely hated being there. One day I walked into the bathroom to take a shower and found a mouse in the bathtub, unable to get out. He slid back down each time he tried to climb out. I called Dad to come and get him out.

Around that time I stopped eating any food at home because I was disgusted by the unsanitary conditions. Mom hardly cleaned the apartment, complaining that cleaning products made her ill, and I found it cynical that she used that as an excuse not to clean the home. According to her, there was nothing doctors could do: no Mr. Clean, Lysol, Fantastic in the home. I was desperate to get out of there. Every now and then, Dad set off one of those bombs used to fumigate roaches, but I never thought that was clever because it didn't get to the source of the infestation.

This is our first apartment in Queens, 94-04 Astoria Boulevard.
The store used to be a candy store owned by Fred and Nellie.

The apartment was sometimes so cold in the winter
that Mom had to turn on the oven in the kitchen for heat.
She left the oven door open to heat the room. She woke us
up for school and had us dress in front of the oven to stay
warm.

Conversely, in the summer it was so hot that I regularly took a shower before going to bed and climbed into bed wet, leaving the window open, and hoped I would fall asleep before the heat got to me. Sometimes the uncomfortable heat awakened me in the middle of the night. All I could do was take a second shower to cool off and jump back into bed wet.

When I was fourteen a few of my uncles took me under their wing. They worked at a couple of supermarkets in midtown Manhattan delivering groceries by van. I only worked with them on Saturdays, the busiest day for grocery deliveries. Mike kept the van at my grandparents' home and agreed to pick me up at our apartment around 6 a.m. so we could get into Manhattan early. Sometimes we took the train into the city. The main supermarket where we worked was at 62nd Street and Second Avenue.

My uncles, Aladino, Mike, and Caesar, had a ritual of having breakfast at the diner at Second Avenue and 63rd Street, at the other end of the street from the supermarket. We typically had a breakfast of eggs, hash brown potatoes, coffee, and toast, and then go to work. It was a special treat for me to eat with them. I always paid for my own breakfast, as we all did. I didn't get any special treatment, which was fine with me.

Working at the supermarket with them was my introduction to the high-end apartments in midtown Manhattan. It was quite impressive to me at fourteen years old to visit the many high-rise apartments, even if it was only to deliver groceries. We used to deliver to people living in places like the St. Regis Hotel, The Pierre, The Carlyle, and many other luxury buildings throughout the city.

That experience was another eye-opener for me. It showed me how nicely people could live, if they made a lot of money. I was impressed to see that you can have your groceries brought to you at home, instead of walking five or six blocks, carrying bags of groceries the way I used to do with Dad.

My pay for this work each Saturday was in tips. I usually made about eight to ten dollars for the day. Just as important as the money, I enjoyed hanging out with my uncles, and I always appreciated that they took me in for that job. The fact is that they really didn't need me. It was a nice gesture on their part, and I learned things that definitely helped me develop a work ethic. It also gave me an appreciation for the socioeconomic differences among people.

There was another lesson I learned in working with them that wasn't so nice, but important just the same. On one delivery, Aladino assigned me to go to the apartment by myself. He said, several times while laughing, that I was obligated to do the delivery by myself and that I could keep the whole tip, rather than putting it in the van's ashtray, where we accumulated the day's tips to distribute amongst the team at the end of the day. I didn't know what he meant by saying I was *obligated* or why he was laughing, but I went to do the delivery, excited that they were letting me keep the whole tip.

When I returned to the van he asked me, while laughing, how much of a tip the lady gave me. The lady did not give me a tip, and he knew she wouldn't. Apparently, she was a regular customer and never tipped. I was not happy! I felt that Aladino intentionally deceived me and it upset me. I never trusted him after that, and I didn't work with them much longer either. That job lasted part of the summer. It wasn't, however, my last job in New York City as a teenager.

Another uncle, Ivan, worked as a delivery man for a butcher on Second Avenue between 63rd and 64th Streets called Albert's. I believe it is still there today as Albert's Prime Meats. Ivan delivered the meat to customers on a bicycle equipped with a basket in the front. I started working with Ivan on Saturdays.

I thought this was a dangerous job because Ivan had to navigate through Manhattan traffic on a bicycle. He was super athletic and was able to zip through traffic, sometimes between the narrowest openings between cars, to get to a destination, while I sat sideways on the bar of the bicycle. Whenever he zipped through a narrow path between cars, I squeezed my legs as close to the bicycle as possible to avoid having my knee caps chopped off, closing my eyes to avoid seeing the inevitable collision. I never told him I was scared because each time I thought we were not going to make it through traffic, Ivan surprised me and got us to the other side. My trust in him to keep us safe in NYC traffic grew with each adventurous Saturday.

Ivan in many respects was my idol. He was four years older than I was, but entered this world on the same day as me. I thought that gave us a special connection. He was also a big-time track star at Newtown High School, with many awards and trophies from events like the Penn Relays. He was great at every sport he played, especially baseball. He tried out for the Pittsburgh Pirates farm system after high school, but didn't make the cut. Still, I was proud of him for being considered by the team.

We celebrated our birthdays together some years. My grandparents didn't do birthday parties for Ivan, and mine didn't for me. When I turned thirteen and fourteen and Ivan seventeen and eighteen, we bought cupcakes at the grocery store to share. We sat on the curb near the store and said happy birthday to each other.

When Ivan decided to stop working at Albert's, the owner hired me to do the deliveries. I worked only on Saturdays since I was in school during the week.

One day when I had completed a delivery near 77th Street and Second Avenue, near Lennox Hill Hospital, where I was born, I got on my bicycle to return to the store. While I was trying to navigate around a city bus that had stopped to pick up and drop off passengers, it started moving sooner than I anticipated, and I was pinned between it and the sidewalk. The bus hit me and knocked me down, crushing the front of the bicycle. I wasn't hurt, and I don't think the bus driver ever saw me, because he never stopped. A lady walking by asked me if I was okay. I told her that I was okay and thanked her for asking. I was clearly not as slick with a bicycle in NYC traffic as Ivan!

I got up and walked the damaged bicycle back to Albert's. With the front tire mangled, I had to lift the bike by the handle bars and walk it down Second Avenue on the rear tire. It was a difficult thirteen or fourteen blocks, but I had no choice. I was not about to leave the bike behind. The store had several bicycles and I was able to use another one to complete my day. I never mentioned the accident to my parents.

I must have had some pretty good angels watching over me to be hit by cars and buses three times in fifteen years and not be badly hurt. I am convinced that these were all lessons put in front of me to define and strengthen my appreciation for life. Why else would I see a young boy get killed by a car after I was grazed by a speeding car? That poor boy was killed and I wasn't hurt. Despite Mom's reaction, it was a lesson that registered in my mind. Interestingly, since I grew up having to see things before I could believe in them, these lessons resonated with me. It was as if God, through my angels, was saying to me, "See what can happen if you are not careful?"

The part I hated about the job at Albert's was riding the bicycle in the rain—it was not at all pleasant to ride through the streets of Manhattan in heavy rain. The bike got heavy and the visibility was poor. After I called Albert on two different rainy Saturdays to say I was not able to work that day, he fired me. I was not at all surprised or upset because I was done there. I was actually relieved that Albert fired me. I knew I had outgrown that experience.

Chapter Twelve

During my early teen years, my best friend in the neighborhood was Jose "Cheo" Martinez. He lived a few blocks from us on 94th Street, near LaGuardia airport. Cheo and his two sisters were raised by an aunt. I never knew what happened to their mother. They never talked about that. I used to hang out with Cheo at their house frequently. That's where I met their father a few times when he went by the house to visit them. I was told he was a merchant marine and traveled constantly.

Cheo, Carmen, and Rosie lived in a large single-family house. Carmen was his older sister, and Rosie the youngest. Carmen began dating Ivan when they were each sixteen. For some reason, Carmen's aunt never liked Ivan.

Cheo's aunt was a practitioner of Santeria, which is a West African and Caribbean religion with customs that include trances to communicate with ancestors and deities, animal sacrifices, and sacred drumming and dances. She was well connected with famous Latin people who frequently visited the house to attend Santeria rituals. I remember seeing on numerous occasions the famous Cuban singer Celia Cruz at the house, and the Puerto Rican singer Bobby Capo. The group dressed in all white from head to toe during ceremonies held at the house.

Sometimes as I walked to and from their house, I stumbled upon heads of chickens on the lawn. Cheo never confessed that they were the remnants of his aunt's religious sacrifices, but I was pretty sure that they were. Whenever I mentioned the chicken heads to Mom, she reacted as if she had the chills, trembling as if to cleanse herself of any evil that might be trying to enter her body. She knew about Santeria, although she did not practice it.

Mom was born in the town of Guayama, Puerto Rico, in 1936. The town has always been known as the city of witches, or *Ciudad de los Brujos*. Guayama has a rich history dominated by native Taino Indian, Spanish, and African influence. It is the combination of Taino and African influence that gave rise to the town's witchcraft history and ultimately its legacy.

Guayama was inhabited by Taino Indians long before Christopher Columbus and Juan Ponce de Leon arrived on the island in 1493. In fact, the name Guayama itself is of Taino origin and means Great Place, or *Sitio Grande* in Spanish. It is noteworthy that the town took its name from a Taino cacique chief who ruled the southeastern region of the island, the Guamani cacique and the Guayama cacique. By the time the first Spanish settlers arrived in 1508, led by Ponce de Leon, the Taino population throughout the island numbered approximately 30,000. By 1514, however, due to the rigors of forced labor by the conquering Spanish and the losses from rebellion, the Taino population dwindled to about 4,000.

With the native population nearly obliterated, the Spanish conquerors introduced African slaves as laborers for the island's growing agriculture industry. Unfortunately, many more Tainos, as well as Spaniards and African slaves, died in 1519 from the smallpox epidemic said to have been brought to the island from Africa.

Nonetheless, the remaining population of Taino Indians and Africans persevered over the centuries. They shared in common spiritual beliefs that grew in rural towns like Guayama into the widespread practice of Espiritismo. Mom was always considered by Grandma and the rest of the family to have been blessed with the special powers to communicate with the spirits of the deceased. The followers of Espiritismo believed that these powers could be used for evil—to cause a spirit to harm someone; or for good—to prevent evil from infiltrating someone's life. Mom considered Santeria to be harmful, and that is why she reacted with a chill when I told her what I had seen outside of Cheo's house.

Mom was the family's Espiritista, communicating with spirits whenever a family member solicited her powers, usually to try to seek help from a spirit who could travel to places where they could not.

As a kid who grew up in New York City, I was never a believer in the practice of Espiritismo. For me it was mostly about tangibility. I did not believe that when Mom's body was possessed by a spirit—speaking in her own voice and not that of the spirit's known voice when he or she was alive—that her body was truly taken over.

Each time Mom awoke from a session where a spirit spoke through her, she fainted and had to be revived with alcohol rubs on her forehead and the back of her neck. She was clearly exhausted and did not remember anything that transpired while she was possessed. Still I was a doubting Thomas, unable and unwilling to believe in what I could not see!

That all changed one afternoon in a chilling fashion…

Ivan and Carmen married after they graduated from high school. I have said before that Carmen and Cheo's aunt, who raised them, did not care for Ivan. I never knew the reason why. Maybe she was just being a possessive parent. They knew they were defying her by getting married, but it is what they wanted. They were in love.

Carmen became pregnant with their first child. The young couple was elated at the blessing they were about to receive. They attended church each Sunday to thank God for the miracle of a child of their very own.

Fast-forward nine months and the devastation that Carmen and Ivan, especially Ivan, experienced when their first child was stillborn. For months they were tormented over their tragedy. Carmen was healthy and did not experience complications during her pregnancy. All of her doctor visits throughout her term produced normal results. Knowing that Carmen's aunt practiced Santeria, Ivan's only practical explanation for the death of their child was that she must have cast an evil spell on them for their defiance.

They visited Mom at our apartment several times to commiserate over their loss, but most importantly to seek confirmation of Ivan's suspicion through Mom's supernatural powers. It was the only way they could find closure for their loss. They did not consider what they would or could do if they were able to confirm that Carmen's aunt was responsible for a demoniac intervention that suffocated their unborn blessing.

Here's where, like doubting Thomas, who came to believe in Jesus only after being blinded for three days and having the Son of God restore his sight, I came to believe in Mom's special gift in being able to connect with the other side.

Carmen had long talked of her older brother who had passed away sometime before our families met. She often spoke of him with glowing and loving memories. On Ivan and Carmen's visit with Mom one afternoon as they sat in the living room talking about their tragedy, Carmen mentioned Tony, her dead brother, and Mom's body shook as if overcome by a cold chill.

Her eyes closed and she stood up. I stepped back to add some distance between us. She asked Ivan and Carmen to stand close in front of her. It was Mom's body, but it was Tony's spirit speaking to them. I watched from a corner of the living room, still skeptical.

The spirit spoke to Carmen and Ivan and told them that he was at the aunt's home at that very moment. As the words emanated from Mom's mouth, the one-way conversation was Tony's spirit speaking to the aunt: "So you're afraid to see me? You know what you did?" he said to her. "Where are you running to? Why are you going upstairs? You know I'm going to follow you." He followed her through the bedrooms on the second floor of the house, as the voice from Mom's mouth described their movements. "Now you want to destroy those pictures you have on the dresser behind that door, but you know that I know what you did."

A few minutes later the event concluded with the confirmation that Ivan and Carmen were seeking.

I had been to that house many times and knew the layout of the rooms downstairs and upstairs. I had walked through the very rooms that the spirit described, but Mom had never been to that house, and even if Carmen or Ivan had by chance described the house to her, they would not have done it at the level of detail that Tony's spirit spoke of. She would not have known where the dresser was positioned, where doors were located, where the aunt's small altar was located, and where she lit candles and placed personal items such as pictures of Ivan and Carmen to share with the evil spirits she summoned to harm them.

Like doubting Thomas two thousand years ago, I was now convinced of Mom's connection to the supernatural. I became a believer!

Chapter Thirteen

Cheo and I attended IS 145 at the same time and frequently played sports together, mostly basketball, at the park we walked to on 90th Street and 31st Avenue. That park was behind elementary school PS 148, where we also played in their afterschool program. We also spent time in the summer at the public Astoria pool to escape the heat.

One day at school we were play fighting in the boys' room with two other kids. It was either in the seventh or eighth grade. During the fight, I swung with my right hand to throw a punch, and Cheo pulled out a box cutter, the type where the blade springs out with the push of a button. He caught my thumb and cut me pretty bad. I ran to the nurse for treatment, and she bandaged my finger and sent me to the principal's office. They questioned me repeatedly to get me to tell them who cut me, but I wouldn't tell. I never divulged that it was Cheo who did it. I didn't want to get him in trouble.

When I got home that afternoon, I showed Mom the cut and told her that my finger was hurting. The deep cut was just above the knuckle on the palm side of my hand, so it was painful when I bent my finger, which often was by reflex. Mom should have taken me for stitches, but she didn't feel well that day and was napping. I walked across Astoria Boulevard to the pharmacy across the street from our apartment, showed the pharmacist my finger, and he sold me some powder to stop the bleeding and some gauze and tape to cover the cut. It wasn't ideal, but I could not go to the hospital myself.

It took a long time to heal, and I still have the scar as a reminder of that day. But I was proud that I never ratted on Cheo. He was my best friend, and even though what he did was stupid and dangerous, I didn't think it was intentional. Cheo and I slowly split apart as we went to different high schools. He went to Bryant High School, where Carmen attended, and I went to Newtown with Ivan.

At IS 145, I began to get involved with other activities that piqued my interest. One was the Spelling Bee contest that, much to my surprise, my English teacher in the seventh grade recommended I enter. I could not believe that someone thought I was smart enough to compete in the spelling bee.

It didn't occur to me to tell Mom or Dad about my participation in the Spelling Bee. I was quietly excited and didn't think they would share in my joy. The first round was during a weekly assembly, and Mr. Smith, an English teacher, was the Master of Ceremonies for the event. He introduced each student, and gave us the words that we had to repeat, spell, and repeat.

The tragedy was that I lost in the first round. I did not hear Mr. Smith properly when he pronounced the word "BAMBOO." I heard him say "BAMPBOO" and that is what I spelled. When I first heard it, I wondered what the word was. It was close to bamboo, which I knew very well, but thought it must be a new word. The entire assembly laughed as I walked off the stage. That was a bit embarrassing, but I was more angry than embarrassed. I was upset that Mr. Smith didn't pronounce the word clearly enough. I wanted a do-over, but that was not possible. I realized then that there is never a second chance to make a first impression.

I had my first foray into politics when I decided to run for Crossing Guard Captain. Nelson, who was in the eighth grade, became captain of the squad and nominated me as sergeant. We had a team of maybe six kids whose mission it was to help other kids cross the streets around the school safely.

For some reason Nelson quit and the rest of the guards asked me to run for the vacant office. I don't remember who ran against me, but I won by a landslide. I had the privilege of wearing the red badge on my crossing guard white rubber belt. I found this to be an honor and was proud of my role.

I was a pretty serious kid who liked to do things correctly, thoroughly, and by the book. Each morning I met with my squad before our tour of duty began. I made sure they wore their belts and badges neatly. We had crossing guard duty in the morning before classes began, at lunch time, and then again in the afternoon when the day was over. I supervised the team to make sure they did their jobs well and made sure students only crossed when the light was green.

One of my guards came back one afternoon with a bloody nose after he was punched by a student whom he tried to stop from jaywalking. I remember hurrying with him and another guard to find the student and "clear up" the matter, but we didn't find him and my guard couldn't remember what he looked like.

I felt terrible that this kid was trying to do his job, the job I asked him to do, and some idiot punched him in the face. Fortunately, that was the only incident we had during my tenure as captain of the guards, which lasted through the eighth grade.

There were plenty of fun times at that school as well. One of those was when the school decided to show a movie during an extended assembly. There we were, Cheo and I, with all of our friends in a darkened theatre at school watching a movie. What a special treat! Our friends included Eric, Derrick, Walter, Jelly, and Paula, all kids from East Elmhurst and Corona.

We decided that we should have some snacks for the movie. How could you go to the movies and not have snacks? The school forbade food in assembly, so we took it upon ourselves to provide it for our group. Cheo and I quietly slid out the side door and walked quickly to White Castle, which was about seven blocks away on Northern Boulevard. We purchased two bags of burgers in their individual boxes and hurried back to school. Eric or Jelly had placed something of a stopper on the door to keep it from locking, so we were able to sneak back in undetected. Even with the smell of burgers in the air, no teacher noticed. Or perhaps they did and decided to let it go.

Some of us pulled this same stunt during an Automotive Shop class. The teacher was a nice older man just trying to get by teaching a bunch of rambunctious seventh- and eighth-grade boys who couldn't care less about auto mechanics. He clearly saw us leaving the class and the building and returning with burgers, but he just let it go.

In 1972, I graduated from IS 145. I was shocked, sad, and angry that my parents did not attend my graduation. Mom always had an excuse that she didn't feel well enough to attend any school event of mine. I thought maybe she was ashamed that she didn't have much education and was therefore uncomfortable in school settings. I thought graduating was an important achievement and at least my mom, if not both my parents, should be there. I craved their moral support and encouragement.

All the students wore caps and gowns in the school's burgundy color for the graduation ceremony at the Boulevard Theatre on Northern Boulevard, a couple of blocks from the school. I bought my own class ring and paid for my cap and gown rental. I was excited to be graduating and looked forward to attending Newtown High School, yet I was incredibly disappointed that no one in my immediate family cared to attend. One of my aunts, Nani, heard that I was graduating and that my parents were not going. She told me she would be happy to attend. I thought that was very kind of her, and it made me happy to have someone from the family there, even if it was not the same as having my parents present.

After the graduation Mom had a cake for me at home to celebrate, and had me put on my cap and gown to take pictures, but the damage was done as far as I was concerned. I didn't want to be unappreciative, but I really wanted her at the ceremony.

When I wasn't in school, I was searching for ways to earn more money. Sometimes it was as simple as volunteering to sell Fred and Nellie's newspapers on days when the candy store was closed. They agreed to let *The Daily News* be delivered when they were on vacation so that I could sell them. On those days I got up early in the morning and sat on the stoop of our building with the pile of newspapers by my side, which I sold to people on their way to the bus stop or to the diner across the street. I held the money and handed it to Fred when they finally returned and opened the store. Fred paid me a buck or two, depending on how many papers I sold.

I remember that one winter during a heavy snowstorm I was looking out of our bedroom window and saw that cars were getting stuck in the snow on Astoria Boulevard right in front of us. Rather than sitting there just looking outside, I thought *Why not make some money helping cars get out of the snow?* I always had a knack for seeing opportunities. We didn't have a shovel at home, so I went to Russell at the deli and borrowed his.

I helped drivers get their cars out of the snow and made more than forty dollars in one day. Most drivers were so elated to be able to drive away that they gave me five dollars. One man gave me a twenty-dollar bill! It was cold, wet, hard work, but it was worth it for a short time of maybe one or two hours.

Whenever none of my friends were around and I was bored, I walked down 94th Street to LaGuardia airport to hang out. It was about five or six blocks away. I sat in the terminal rest areas and watched travelers walk by, or gazed at the airplanes through the floor-to-ceiling windows as they landed and took off. I fantasized about being a businessman and traveling the world. Over time that fantasy became one of my life's missions. I walked into the shops and browsed through books and magazines, spying on businessmen and women to see what books and magazines they were purchasing.

I was on an airplane only once in thirteen years. When Mom was eight months pregnant with Susan, she took the four of us to Mayaguez, Puerto Rico, where she wanted Susan to be born. The four of us were born on the mainland, and she wanted her last planned child to be born on the island. Dad had to work, so he stayed home.

The plan to have Susan born in Mayaguez didn't materialize, however. Within a week of being there, Mom had an argument with my grandmother. Agitated, Mom packed all our things and we took a flight back to New York. Susan was born two weeks later on June 15, 1963 in New York City.

I enjoyed the airport because it was exciting to fantasize about traveling, getting on a plane, and going to different places. It was very different back in the early 1970s. The security measures between then and now are like night and day. Back then, anyone could walk through security and go all the way to any gate. I was able to walk to a gate, sit there watching the passengers get on board, and eventually see the flight take off. It gave me a new goal in life. I vowed that one day I would be a world traveler.

I spent so much time at LaGuardia airport that I was able to see and meet some celebrities. One evening when I was hanging out at one of the gates, I saw the entire Philadelphia Phillies baseball team standing there waiting to board their flight. They were in town playing the New York Mets, and Shea Stadium was almost walking distance from the airport, and from our apartment. I didn't recognize any of the players, but I approached them to get an autograph. Unfortunately, none would give me one.

My most memorable encounter was one afternoon as I walked through the airport near the ticket counter and I noticed Bob Hope walking by himself. It was the middle of a warm sunny day, and he wore a dark suit and carried a briefcase. He walked right past me. I decided to hurry back and ask him for his autograph, which he graciously gave to me. I was thrilled, not so much for having the piece of paper with Bob Hope's signature, but because he was gracious. I will always have the memory of meeting Bob Hope one on one, even if I no longer have his autograph. I didn't mention that I got Bob Hope's autograph to my parents. I placed the piece of paper with his signature on top of our refrigerator and never saw it again. It must have been thrown out with the garbage.

On a different afternoon I saw Colonel Sanders, the founder and image of Kentucky Fried Chicken, walking through the airport. Up until then, I thought that his all-white suit and black string tie were only an image for television and billboard commercials, but he looked every bit the part of the original colonel. It turns out that for the last twenty years of his life, from 1960 to 1980, all he wore in public was his white suit and black string tie, with matching white hair, mustache, and goatee.

Another summer afternoon, while walking to the airport, I met Tug McGraw outside his home on 94th Street near Ditmars Boulevard, across the street from the Traveler's Hotel. It must have been his in-season home while pitching for the New York Mets. I walked up to Tug and got his autograph.

I was born a New York Yankees fan, having grown up during my early years in the Bronx. But living about two miles from Shea Stadium on Astoria Boulevard, I also became a Mets fan. My uncle Mike even took me to one of the World Series games in 1969.

Chapter Fourteen

In the early 1970s my parents were arguing quite a bit.

One afternoon while I was at home they had a fight, and Dad was trying to hold Mom down on their bed. She was screaming hysterically because she knew that my uncle Ivan was outside waiting for me to meet him downstairs. She ran to the window screaming that Dad had hit her, which was not true. She expected that my uncle would come upstairs and beat up my dad or somehow save her.

I was there and know that Dad did not hit her. He was just trying to calm her down. I remember Dad looking scared and saying that he had not hit her, that he was just holding her. Luckily, neither Ivan nor anyone else interfered. This was a time of great pain and confusion at home, and it had a negative impact on many people. Shortly after that argument, Mom did something that I had a difficult time understanding then, and am saddened by even now.

While Dad was at work, my mom had absolutely everything in the apartment packed, and we moved to another apartment on 111th Street in Corona, in a two-family detached home next to a school. We moved into the second-floor apartment. Mom told all five of us not to tell anyone where we lived, even though my uncle Lito moved us there, and so that part of the family had to know where we lived. In fact, my uncles Caesar, Ivan, and Mike came over a couple of times so we could play softball on the nearby school's asphalt ball field.

I remember Mom telling me to run away if I saw my dad on the street. She knew that I walked the streets of the old neighborhood and was concerned that I might let my dad know where we lived. The area where we now lived was not far from the Junction Boulevard number 7 train station, and that is where he caught the train to go to work in Long Island City. It was also the station where I used to catch the train into the city.

I was saddened and confused by this episode, and by the thought that Dad was to come home the day we moved out, only to see the apartment entirely cleaned out and all of us gone. That quickly, and for no good reason that I could think of, Mom took away his whole family and didn't leave him a chair to sit on or a bed to sleep in. Maybe their confrontation had been her informing him that she was going to move out?

Although I went about my daily routine—school, hanging out with friends, visiting with my girlfriend, Cynthia—this episode in my family's life was impactful. Mom was a woman and as such taught me, through actions such as this, that a man had to guard against being hurt by a woman.

I thought this was a cruel and cowardly thing she had done. Rather than facing whatever problems they had, she decided to run away from it and hurt all of us in the process. I suspected that she was hiding a dark secret and preferred to leave rather than be exposed.

It was irresponsible of her to tell us not to speak to my dad if we saw him on the street. I never spoke to my brothers and sisters about this and I'm sure they all remember this event, but I don't know how it has affected them. By instructing us not to speak to Dad, and to run away if he saw us, Mom made us pawns in the middle of their battle. That was both irresponsible and damaging.

A selfish person does not by their very nature have the capacity to consider what impact their behavior will have on others. Their behavior is generally uncalculated, impulsive. The only thing that matters to them is what they want. An adult who is unselfish, giving of his time and resources, can recognize a selfish, self-absorbed person and can choose to avoid a relationship with that person. A young son or daughter does not have that privilege.

We are captive students, absorbing all that our parents teach us, good or bad. Who will be there later in our lives to help us unravel the bad from the good, and purge the bad from our repository of experiences?

The chaotic episode proved to be another lesson in integrity and trust or, more accurately, the lack of it. It's unfortunate to say that, but it is what it is.

As my luck would have it, one afternoon I walked up the stairs of the Junction Boulevard train station, and as I neared the turnstile I saw Dad walking through the door. He had gotten off the train and was on his way home. I thought it was much too early; he usually came home in the late evening. He must have changed his work hours or, unable to concentrate, left work early. He must have been worried about what happened to us and where we might be.

As soon as I saw him, I could tell that he was having a difficult time. He looked sad. I saw that his eyes were red, and I assumed it was from crying and lack of sleep. He also looked thinner than usual. This was only one week after we left home. We walked down the stairs together, and he asked me how I was and if I was hungry. As we walked down Junction Boulevard past the train station, he said he wanted to give me money to give to Mom.

He did not ask me where we were living, but I felt that was coming. It made me sad to see my dad hurting, and the mere memory of that encounter brings tears to my eyes. I felt anger at Mom for putting us all in this position to satisfy her selfish interests. I was very confused, remembering that she had instructed us to run away if we saw Dad, yet I was glad to see him. And I felt sad to see him go through this ordeal. I made a sudden decision that I would run away and do as Mom had instructed. I turned around and bolted back toward the train station. I lost Dad as I ran through Corona. Mom had prevailed! I felt terrible having to do that, and angry at the same time. When I got home I told Mom I had seen Dad and run away. She was glad that I did.

For some reason that Mom never explained to us, within two weeks she decided we would move back home with Dad. This was yet another confusing event for all of us. Within two weeks she emptied the apartment, left our dad, and then returned. What was this all about? It made me angry and taught me that if I could not trust my mom, I should not trust anyone. This episode only served to further compound the general mistrust growing inside of me.

I recall visiting my grandparents' home a few blocks away sometime after we returned home, and listening to my grandmother scold me for having run away from my dad. I didn't care much for her opinion. She was talking to the wrong person, I thought. She should have been scolding her daughter, my mom, not me. I was put in the middle of this so my mom could protect herself. My dad never scolded me for running away from him, but I suspect that he held that against me for a long time.

Having thought over the years again and again about this episode from my early teenage years, I know it has shaped the way I strive to treat people, especially when faced with a problem. I figure that it is much more damaging to run away from a problem than to face it and deal with it openly and directly. Running away from a problem ends up creating guilt, shame, and regret; it damages, perhaps irreversibly, relationships and fosters a pattern lacking in integrity.

There is no question in my mind that the best policy to resolve any conflict is to address it quickly, respectfully, and directly. It is important to avoid personal attacks and condescension. That is a philosophy, an approach, I learned the hard way over the years and not something I was necessarily taught. Being upfront may not always be easy because it requires a confrontation, but it will more often than not clear the air of controversy.

After we returned home to Astoria Boulevard, Dad began doing things to earn extra money. On weekends he sold *piraguas*, shaved ice cones in paper cups sweetened with different fruit-flavored syrups.

He inherited a wooden piragua cart from my uncle William, who had one in the South Bronx and brought it to Queens when we all moved there. Once in Queens, he began working other businesses like making costume jewelry and gave the piragua cart to Dad.

I helped him by getting the ice whenever he needed a block. He sent me with three quarters to the sidewalk ice dispenser a few blocks east on Astoria Boulevard to pick up a block of ice, and each time I took a towel to drape over one shoulder so that the large block would not slide off and hit the ground. The towel also limited the melting ice from dripping all over my clothing. It was summertime, so I had to hurry home to preserve as much of the ice as possible. Dad helped me lift the block onto the center of the cart and draped the towel over it to protect it from the sun. Each time someone stopped by to order a piragua, he peeled off the towel (it literally stuck to the ice), shaved the ice, fit it into the paper cup, and poured the customer's requested flavor.

When he wasn't selling piraguas, Dad worked at Mr. Butts' real estate office around the corner from our apartment doing sundry jobs for the owner. Sometimes that included cleaning out a house that Mr. Butts had purchased and needed cleaned before he could sell it. Once, Dad took me to a mansion in Jamaica Estates, and I was amazed by how large the house was. He wanted me to help him clean the place, but I was too distracted by the enormity of the residence I found myself in. I was amazed that while we lived in a cramped apartment, another family could live in a house so large that you could hear your echo in the empty hallway.

It was yet another of the numerous experiences that influenced my future. I daydreamed about living in a large home someday. Having no real idea what effort it required, I started saving money with the intention of having enough to one day rent my very own apartment. Of course, at fourteen I was too young to do that. Still, it gave me a sense of purpose that helped me move my life forward.

Meanwhile, I was so angry with my parents that I began to be more rebellious. I was hanging out at the 90th Street Park later into the night. When I wasn't at the park, I was staying in the Bronx. I had a girlfriend, Robin Wolfson, who lived with her parents in the north Bronx on Ollinville Avenue, near Allerton Avenue. Robin had a twin sister, Andrea, and a younger brother, Paul. Her mom, Helene, liked me, and since her husband left them to move to Florida with a mistress, she was okay with me staying in their home.

They lived in a nice, clean, comfortable apartment on the tenth floor of a well-maintained building. The building had elevators and their apartment had air-conditioning and a terrace that overlooked a small playground and sitting area below. Those were amenities that I was not accustomed to, but quickly grew to appreciate. Their home provided a welcome escape from the apartment that I lived in, with no air-conditioning to provide relief from sweltering heat in the summer and broken boilers that too often resulted in bone-chilling cold in the winter. My experience visiting, and sometimes staying there, gave me another taste of how differently I could live. They had a three-bedroom, two-bathroom apartment with a dining area that was separate from the kitchen. Most of all, it was clean with no roaches or mice. In my home we never had a dining room, and only one bathroom to share among seven of us. I thought having two bathrooms was a luxury.

When my girlfriend's mom suggested I stay overnight so I did not have to take the subway late at night to Queens, I was thrilled. Surprised, but thrilled. Astonished that a mom invited a teenage boy to stay in her apartment with her daughter, but thrilled! Helene often visited with neighbors in the evenings to watch *The Tonight Show* on television, and Paul hibernated in his bedroom, so Robin and I were often alone in the apartment—at least for a few hours until Helene came home from down the hall.

Whenever I got home the next day after staying at Robin's, Mom asked me where I had been. I usually told her I was at Robin's, but sometimes I rebelliously said simply that I was out. By this time at fourteen and fifteen years of age, the abuse I felt at home was less physical and more emotional. I was getting too big and vocal for my parents to beat me. They had lost control of me. As I separated from them, by spending less and less time at home, sometimes not even coming home to sleep, they started to see that I was different and not willingly follow-ing in their footsteps.

They liked the fact that I was working. It enabled them to benefit from my financial contribution to the family. They felt it was my duty to work for them, so my giving Mom a portion of my earnings, little as it might have been, made them happy. Still, we frequently had arguments over money and what they wanted from me. They wanted me to work to give them money, and I wanted to work to fund my education and otherwise support myself.

I felt it was a big help to them that by my working to partially support myself (I still lived under their roof), they did not have to buy my school supplies, clothing, or even food. I stopped eating at home because I was disgusted with how dirty the apartment was. My diet consisted of fast foods like pizza, McDonald's, Jack in the Box, or an affordable charbroiled burger and fries or one scrambled egg and mashed potatoes at the Star Diner across the street from our apartment. For the Thanksgiving and Christmas holidays, I was usually invited to dinner at Robin's home. If her family was invited to a holiday dinner at a relative's home, they always invited me to go along with them. I was happy to celebrate the holidays with them. Robin's family was my second family. I think Helene knew that I craved a family life and she was happy to take me in.

One afternoon I arrived at their apartment around 5 p.m. and was surprised that Helene and Robin had prepared a dinner of spaghetti and meatballs, salad, and oven-warmed rolls as a special dinner for me. I couldn't believe they did that—just for me. We all sat in the dining room for dinner—like a family.

One afternoon, Robin came to Queens to visit me. I met her at the Junction Boulevard train station, and we walked the eight or so blocks to my parents' apartment. Mom was upset that afternoon. She was complaining about us kids not paying attention to her. I think she was experiencing anxiety because her children were separating from her as they grew into teenagers, especially Nelson and me. It was bad timing to have Robin visit, but I did not know that ahead of time. I had no idea she would explode while Robin was there. All of a sudden she threw a bottle of ketchup against the wall in the living room. There was red, blood-like ketchup and glass everywhere. I was embarrassed that Robin had to see how ridiculous and childish my mom could be. It was a demonstration of aggression she had not seen before in her own home. When I saw the fear in her eyes, I hurried her out of there and we headed back to the Bronx. I thought Mom threw that tantrum in retaliation. She was not happy that I was spending all my free time with Robin and not with her. She was jealous. But she had lost the ability to frighten me. Her behavior only served to fuel the anger festering inside of me. I was already feeling independent.

As a further expression of my independence, the summer of 1972 after I turned fifteen years old, I went to the DMV office in Jamaica, Queens, and obtained a learner's permit. I wanted to learn to drive correctly, so I immediately signed up with a driving school. After taking the six required hands-on driving lessons, I went for the road test and passed. I became the first person in our home to have a driver's license. I was proud of myself, but I was alone in that as well. Mom and Dad didn't care.

My next mission was to save enough money to one day purchase a car. In the meantime, Uncle Lito gladly rented a car for me whenever I asked. He and I went to one of the nearby rental car agencies, of which there were several since we lived close to LaGuardia airport, and I paid him for the rental and made sure I was careful driving. I felt the extra incentive to protect his name since he had signed for the car. We did this on occasional weekends, and I drove the rental to the Bronx to hang out there with Robin.

Robin's dad, Stanley, had a brand-new, beautiful Cutlass Supreme. Once when he was traveling, he left his car parked in the apartment building's lot. I think he was traveling to Florida visiting his mistress, so Helene was feeling down and wanted to go out. She knew I had my driver's license and that I drove a rental car from my borough to theirs.

That weekend I arrived at their apartment on the subway. It was a sunny Saturday afternoon and Helene wanted to enjoy a day outdoors. She did not drive, so she suggested that I drive Stanley's car and take her, Robin, and Paul to the South Street Seaport. I was happy to oblige. We had an enjoyable afternoon in the city and soon the car was back in its designated parking spot—not a scratch on it.

My parents were indifferent to my having a driver's license. In fact, I believe they saw this as another example of how different I was. Mom sometimes commented that Nelson was a great driver, even though he didn't have a license to drive. But she never praised me for my achievement in getting my learner's permit, taking the initiative to sign up for the driving lessons, passing the road test the first time, and getting my license. It was as if she was minimizing my achievement by praising Nelson's driving skills. It was symbolic. I thought that she praised something done the quick, easy way, rather than the proper way. It bothered me, but it didn't deter me from continuing to pursue my independence and charting my own path forward.

Although I was only fifteen and technically not supposed to work full time, I talked my way into a job at Jack in the Box, which was within walking distance from home, on Astoria Boulevard around 81st Street, across the street from a McDonald's. I was on a mission to make lots of money, so I was ecstatic to get that job.

My schedule at Newtown High School during the ninth and tenth grades was from noon to 5 p.m., so I started working at Jack in the Box from 6 to 11 p.m. I managed to do my homework in the morning before going to school. I worked more hours on Saturday and Sunday, as many as ten hours each day. After finishing my night at work, I hopped on the subway and headed to Robin's home in the Bronx. Sometimes that was as early as 6 a.m., riding the number 7 Flushing Line after the graveyard shift.

My managers at Jack in the Box were impressed with my work ethic, and gave me as many hours as I wanted to work. I was careful not to sacrifice my school-work my first and second years at Newtown. On Friday and Saturday I usually worked the graveyard shift, from 8 p.m. to 6 a.m., closing the restaurant and doing the cleaning with the rest of the crew. During the summer, after we finished cleaning and prepared the restaurant for the morning shift, we climbed the stairs to the roof and slept in the open air for an hour or so (working nights was tiring), or we sat in the dining room and had breakfast, usually in cold weather. By the time I was sixteen, I was promoted to shift manager and was responsible for the graveyard shift.

My first manager was a 6'7" man named Ron. He was another role model for me. I saw Ron as a successful businessman and liked his style of work. He seemed to love Jack in the Box, and was on a fast track with the company. Within a year of my working there, he was promoted to regional manager, responsible for a number of restaurants in the Northeast; from Gun Hill Road in the Bronx, to our location in Jackson Heights, Queens, the one on Junction Boulevard in Corona, and a few others.

One evening, I was working at the restaurant when Ron came barging in from his Lefrak City home around 1 a.m. He called me to the upstairs office and seemed rather pissed off, and I had no idea why. He began scolding me in a calm, but strong voice. Apparently, his mistress, Renee, who also worked there, for some reason had told him that I mentioned to her that I was going to tell his wife they were having an affair. Renee clearly did not like me. Maybe it was because she was jealous that I was made shift manager and she wasn't. She never told me what her problem was with me. Not only did I never say that to Renee, but I didn't even know Ron's wife, their home phone number, or address. I could only guess that Renee told him that lie to get me fired.

I was shocked and upset by the allegation! I told Ron that I had no idea what she was talking about. "I am working fifty hours a week, going to school full time, and have no time to do anything else, much less talk to Renee about a relationship I know nothing about." He saw how genuinely upset I was and he must have believed me, so he apologized and left to go home.

I never saw them together as lovers, but I could only surmise that they were having sex in the office because they often stayed up there for long periods of time with the door locked. When they finished whatever they were doing and opened the door, anyone walking by could see a sheet of white cleaning cloths on the floor. That was the only real clue I had that they were doing something on the floor. But, it wasn't my concern.

I was excited that I was seen as a leader and given what I felt were leadership responsibilities. Those were my priorities at the time. Everything else was useless noise.

In an effort to improve service and appearance at its stores, Jack in the Box management implemented a contest to find the best store in each of its regions. The metrics included: cleanliness of the dining room and the kitchen, neatness in the parking lot, including no overflowing garbage cans and a neat Dumpster, quality and freshness of the food, and quick turnaround time at the cash register and the drive-thru. The latter was of special concern to management, and they placed greater weight on that metric.

At the drive-thru, each car had to consume a maximum of two minutes, from the time the customer placed their order, to the time they paid. A drive-thru customer's order had to be taken within ten seconds of the bell ringing, signaling a customer's arrival. We never knew when a customer coming through the drive-thru might be a management employee judging the customer experience.

Among all its restaurants in the Northeast, mine won when my shift was best in all the categories. I was invited, at sixteen years old, to the regional managers' meeting to be presented with the award. I was very proud. This was simply the result of my focus on being the best at whatever I did, as well as my need for recognition.

My parents never knew of this achievement. I didn't tell them because I knew they would not understand or care. At least that was the impression I grew to develop. The managers at Jack in the Box appreciated my work and recognized and rewarded my ambition. That was enough recognition for me! I was very happy there! For the duration of my shift, I was in control of my surroundings. I was in control of the cleanliness of the restaurant, the quality of the food, even the attire of my team. I made sure everyone looked good with clean shirts and hats, and that customers were treated well. I did very well there because I was allowed to flourish. I also worked with some good people, even with a future celebrity.

One friend I met there was Eddie. He lived a block away from our apartment, alone in a basement apartment, although his parents lived around the corner. Eddie was a phenomenal basketball player. He was short at about 5'7", but he was super quick. Whenever we were not working, we would find some time to play basketball at the park on 90th Street or at PS 127. Eddie didn't miss too many jump shots or layups. He had quit high school, so he worked many hours to make as much money as possible. He was such a good basketball player that I tried to get him to re-enroll at school, thinking he would do well on the Newtown High School basketball team. He wasn't interested in school and wouldn't go for my idea. We remained friends for years until I moved away from the area.

Chapter Fifteen

Rita Tellone worked with me at Jack in the Box in 1973 or 1974. She also went to Newtown High School with me. Rita was tall and beautiful. She and her family lived in a very nice Tudor-style row house in Jackson Heights. Her dad drove a yellow taxi, and I think her mom stayed at home raising the four girls.

At Jack in the Box the employees didn't have a changing room, so we all used the low-ceilinged supply room upstairs, where the soda tanks were located, along with the soda syrup boxes and all the other nonperishable supplies. One day I saw Rita changing her shirt in the room. She knew I was there, and didn't mind that I was seeing her with just her bra on.

I remembered that scene later when I saw her on the cover of *Penthouse* magazine. She went on to become a very successful fashion model. In addition to *Penthouse*, she appeared on the covers of *Cosmopolitan* and *Sports Illustrated* and in the film *Eyes of Laura Mars* with Faye Dunaway and Tommy Lee Jones. It was an inspiration to me to walk into a newsstand in Corona, where we had been living at the time, and see, on the cover of *Penthouse* or *Cosmopolitan*, someone from the neighborhood—someone I knew during our adolescent years and went to school with, rode the bus with to and from school, and worked with at Jack in the Box. It gave me the feeling that I could do something and be successful in life just like Rita Tellone. She was always a nice girl and I was very happy for her.

During my freshman year at Baruch College, I majored in journalism and worked at the school newspaper, *The Ticker*. I had a part-time job at a law firm on Wall Street, Davis Polk & Wardwell. I worked there a few hours a day helping with office maintenance. One day, I went into an empty office and called Rita. I wanted to interview her and submit the article to *Latin NY*, a magazine that was popular at the time among Latinos in the city, especially Puerto Ricans.

Rita answered the phone and we talked for a few minutes about her career. I wanted to know about her experience in the movie *Eyes of Laura Mars*. I knew she had a small part, but was surprised when she told me she was paid only $900 for her role. I wrote the article and submitted it to *Latin NY*. An editor called me and said she liked the article, but wanted to suggest some changes and asked me to resubmit it. I said I would, but got busy with school and work and never resubmitted the article.

A few other successful celebrities came out of our neighborhoods. I knew John Leguizamo from hanging out at the 90th Street Park. John was a funny, happy-go-lucky kid who was usually joking with everyone and went on to be a very successful actor. My younger brother, Wil, knew him better than I did. He was younger than the guys I hung out with, closer in age to Wil. Of course, it gave me a sense of pride to see his one-man show *Freak* on Broadway. I could easily recall the faces of the friends he was talking about in that show as if they were in front of me in that theater. I could identify with his stories and found the show very entertaining.

One of our other friends from the neighborhood who knew John pretty well was Joey Vazquez, who had gone on to become a corrections officer at Riker's Island. He also went to see *Freak* and was excited to see John there and decided to get his attention backstage. He passed a note to an usher to give to John, and when he didn't get a reply, he was upset that John ignored him. Joey was a nice guy, but also temperamental and excitable. It didn't occur to him that maybe the usher never gave the note to John.

I ran into John years later at Patria on 18th Street and Park Avenue in New York City, a Nuevo Latino restaurant that was popular with upper-middle-class Latinos and others who enjoyed Caribbean food. I was sitting at the bar, and John and a group of five friends were sitting at a table behind me. When they finished their dinner, John went to the restroom. He was expecting to meet his friends at their table when he returned, but the table was empty. His friends had decided to play a trick on him and pretend they had left the restaurant. For an instant, John had this confused look on his face, wondering what happened to his group. Suddenly, they appeared from behind a column to surprise him. True to his personality, he simply laughed as they walked out.

Carlos Ferreira was another friend who I got to hang out with during the summers. He was friends with Cheo also, and often the three of us played basketball together. Carlos was a role model for me and a kid I was proud of. While I was still in high school, Carlos was attending the University of Kansas, studying law. When the school year was over, he returned home to the neighborhood for the summer. Once the summer was over, Carlos was off to Kansas. I thought it was pretty cool that I knew someone who was going to be a lawyer.

From about the time I was sixteen, I realized that I did not like authority figures. I disliked being told what to do. I preferred to be asked, or coached, to do something. My upbringing and the lack of trust I had in my parents made me suspicious of any authority figure, especially those who tried to boss me around or bully me. I was successful at Jack in the Box because the managers were mentors as opposed to bosses. I was lucky to start out with them because it afforded me the opportunity to flourish in my first formal job.

As part of this first formal job, I now had to learn to deal with filing an income tax return. The first year, my dad suggested that he prepare it for me...for five dollars. It was insulting, especially considering that all along I had been giving money to my mom. I thought he was greedy and inconsiderate, but I didn't have another option, so I let him prepare them. It turned out to be a horror story.

The first year I paid him the five dollars as soon as I received my refund. The following year I noticed that he anticipated when my refund was scheduled to arrive, and watched the mail delivery to see if the check was in the box. I didn't like that he was pressuring me. It was almost comical to see him rushing downstairs to the mailbox around the time the mailman usually delivered our mail to try to beat me to it—for five dollars. He wanted to get my refund check to force me to pay him. He even tried to collect from me, telling me I should pay him because it was *his* five dollars. To me it was childish and downright silly, but that is how he was about money.

I was so defiant that I did not pay him, and learned to prepare my own return on the EZ form. When I realized how easy it was, it just confirmed to me how ridiculous it was that he was charging his own son five dollars for the five-minute effort. It would have been more appropriate for him to show me how to fill out the form. This only increased my suspicion of figures of authority as sneaky, greedy, and manipulative. It was due to this dislike of authority figures that I stopped working at Jack in the Box on Astoria Boulevard.

After Ron was promoted to regional manager, a new manager came on board. Ashraf, a Pakistani man, was authoritative and manipulative, and he habitually insisted that I work extra hours with no advance notice. Often it was to relieve another employee who was a friend of his. I found out that he and Bob, also from Pakistan, were then going out to socialize.

Initially, I didn't mind because the additional hours increased my paycheck. However, once I noticed that Ashraf was taking advantage of my willingness to work, I refused to stay longer beyond my scheduled hours, or work on my scheduled day off when he asked. I especially declined when I saw that it was only so he and Bob could go hang out.

On the last occasion that he asked me to stay beyond my scheduled time, Ashraf and I argued about it and I quit the job on the spot, leaving him to cover my shift. He was so angry that when I showed up a few days later to pick up my paycheck, he threw it on the ground in front of me. I suppose that was his way of telling me that I was garbage.

I thought about leaving it there and asking him to just mail it to me, but decided not to argue any further with him. I picked up my check and left. I have often joked with friends that I was keeping an "F.U." list to one day send a gold embossed Cartier or Tiffany card to each person on that list to simply say, "F.U." Ashraf, wherever he may be today, was the first person on my list, although he is not worth the gold lettering that would be on the card.

During the early 1970s, street gangs began to show up in the parks where we hung out. When I was sixteen years old, I was searching for self-fulfillment to fill the void created by a lack of a family closeness at home. Robin's family filled some of that void, but somehow it wasn't enough. Perhaps it was because they were different from me. They were Jewish and I was Puerto Rican. I loved them for welcoming me into their home and their family, but it wasn't filling the void completely.

I began to hang out more and more with members of the Latin Tops, a Puerto Rican gang that started out in Greenpoint, Brooklyn, and made its way out to Jackson Heights, Queens. I became a member of the gang after a group of them came to my rescue in a confrontation I had with a group of black kids in East Elmhurst.

One night, at about 10 p.m., I was walking near 101st Street and Curtis Street, on my way home from my girlfriend Cynthia's house, when a group of three or four black kids approached me and demanded money. They took the one dollar I had in my pocket. I was so angry I vowed to get back at them. I assumed they picked on me because I was a Puerto Rican kid walking in a black neighborhood.

They also probably didn't like that a Puerto Rican kid was visiting a black girl in their neighborhood. Cynthia Lester was my very first girlfriend when I was fourteen years old, and remained a good friend on and off for more than fifteen years. When she heard what had happened, she confronted the kids on the street.

The day following my encounter with the street punks, I mentioned what had happened to some of the Latin Tops gang members at the 90th Street Park. To my surprise, they immediately committed to finding the guys and "fixing" the situation for me. The gang was led by Louie, a muscular Puerto Rican.

That evening we headed to East Elmhurst in a car to find the guys who had harassed and robbed me. Once we were already in the car and moving, I found out that the burgundy Pontiac Riviera was a stolen car. I thought, *Oh, great!* I was scared that we might get stopped by the police and arrested. To top it off some of the guys were carrying weapons. Luckily, we did not get stopped by the police, and made it to Cynthia's block. We stopped at her house to say hello, and walked the streets looking for the guys, but we never found them.

Soon after that I broke up with Cynthia and began dating Robin, a girl in the Bronx who Nelson introduced me to.

The very fact that the guys were willing to protect me gave me a feeling of comfort. It was the first time that I felt I had a group of people who wanted to look out for me. I joined the gang as a member and spent more time hanging out with them. Occasionally, we got into fights with other gangs at the 90th Street Park, but nothing serious. The police started patrolling the park frequently to keep us out of trouble.

The gang was more about having a close-knit group that protected each other, hung out at parties, and visited other parks to hang out. It gave us a feeling of strength in numbers. It was also like having a family that I did not have at home.

The most serious near-confrontation we were involved in was when the Latin Tops were scheduled to have a rumble with another gang in Flushing. About thirty of us got on the Flushing Line train at Junction Boulevard and headed to a park to meet up with the other gang. We waited by the token booth until we heard the train arriving at the station, then we walked through the door of the station and ran up to the platform to board the train. Guys were carrying knives, a guy we called Turkey had a golf club, and others carried baseball bats. Ever since my encounter with the punks in East Elmhurst, I had started carrying a large knife with a blade about eight inches long. That is what I carried that day.

The police somehow got word that there might be trouble in Flushing, and they intercepted us at the park and made sure we did not get into a fight. The rumble never took place and we headed back to our base park.

At Newtown High School I met Ernie, who lived in a single-family house on my grandparents' block. Ernie had a denim jacket with the colors on the back of another South Bronx gang, the Royal Javelins. I thought the jacket was cool and wanted to see about becoming a member of that gang. One afternoon walking home from school with Ernie, I asked him who the Royal Javelins were. He invited me to visit the gang's hangout in the Bronx. One evening before I went to see Robin, Ernie took me to the Royal Javelins' clubhouse.

Their club was in a storefront with blacked-out windows. Inside there was a beige couch, a table, and a few chairs. There were two or three girls sitting around, and some guys, all members of the gang. I was led into a second room where the leader, a guy named Luis, introduced himself. I think it was the infamous leader of the gang, Luis Lugo, who later in life became a New York City corrections officer. Everyone was pleasant and I felt comfortable.

Luis told me that the initiation for me to join the gang would be lashes with a whip on my bare back. He asked me to take my shirt off and face the wall with my arms stretched out on the wall. I clenched my teeth and waited for the first lash. It hurt, but I was used to that pain from beatings I had gotten from my mom and dad.

After the second lash, Luis said he had one more coming. After I responded that it was cool, he said that because I was okay with it, he would not whip me again. That was it and I was now a Royal Javelin, making me a member of two gangs. I put my shirt back on, said good-bye to the guys, and headed out to meet Robin. She was pretty upset when I told her what I had just done, especially when she saw the red, raw scars on my back.

The experience with the gangs was at a point in my life when I was feeling alone and empty. They filled a void inside me.

As an act of rebellion, and influenced by my surroundings, I was missing many days from school. During my junior year at Newtown High School, I remember missing forty-five days in one semester. My parents had no clue about this because they never paid attention to my schoolwork. My rebelling was sort of "if they don't care if I go to school, why go?" Nelson had dropped out in the ninth grade, and they were okay with that. If they didn't care, I wouldn't either. I later realized that I was lashing out at Mom and Dad, but ultimately hurting myself. Luckily, that discovery came soon enough such that it prevented me from getting into serious trouble.

I remember going back to school one day, and in gym class the teacher called me out. I expected him to scold me for missing so many days from school, but instead he applauded in front of the entire class and thanked me for showing up after being absent forty-five days. I was quite embarrassed and felt I had made a spectacle of myself. Perhaps that was his point. If it was, he made the proper impression on me. But my reaction to that display came in two stages.

Having reached my lowest point in school, I went to Mom and asked her to take me out. I didn't want to go anymore. The strange thing was that both she and Dad were quite okay if we kids wanted to drop out of school. That became hard for me to understand, but I tried it. They were jeopardizing our future, but didn't see it. In a strange way it must have given them a sense of pride that their kids wanted to drop out of school just like they did years before. They had already allowed Nelson to drop out, so I knew they would do the same for me.

Mom more than gladly went to Newtown with me and signed me out of school. I had become a dropout. The more I thought about it, the more I felt it was sad that they could never attend a school event to offer encouragement, but could so easily bring my school education to an end.

The day she went with me to sign me out was the only time my mom had visited my high school.

I wasn't working at that time and spent my days hanging out in the park, or in the Bronx with Robin. I saw my friend Cheo, who had gone to Bryant High School after IS 145, drop out as well. Cheo was doing nothing with his life at the time. He was hanging out and drinking alcohol, and I wasn't pleased with what I saw. Other friends were starting to get into trouble and do time in prison. Two guys we used to hang out with were arrested for burglarizing a lady's home in Corona, stealing guns from her home, and murdering a neighborhood bully whom none of us liked. We were sad to see them arrested because they did everyone in the neighborhood a favor by killing the bully who terrorized many kids. They shot him while he walked in a park on 96th Street and Roosevelt Avenue, just two blocks from where we lived.

Chapter Sixteen

After approximately four years living in East Elmhurst, at 94th Street and Astoria Boulevard, we moved to an apartment in Corona, on 94th Street and Roosevelt Avenue. It was just a few feet away from the train station steps and under the EL.

The apartment was a two-bedroom, one-bathroom unit above a store, similar to the one we had just left at 94-04 Astoria Boulevard. The one difference was that there was a separate room in the hall that you could get to by walking up the stairs and turning a sharp right without entering the apartment. This must have been a storage room for the store downstairs, but the landlord let us keep it as part of the apartment.

My parents allowed me to use that room as my bedroom. The room was completely bare and did not have a closet or heat. That didn't matter to me—I was thrilled that I could have privacy and stay away from the rest of the family. I didn't eat at home anymore, so I didn't need to go to the kitchen. The only bad part was when I had to use the bathroom, which required that I go to the main apartment and through the living room. Other than that, I was pretty much isolated, which I liked.

I made that room my oasis, of sorts. I installed a telephone of my very own, and put a padlock on the door so no one would get in when I was away. I also purchased a portable heater for the winter. My parents equipped the room with a twin bed, a light metal closet, and a small dresser.

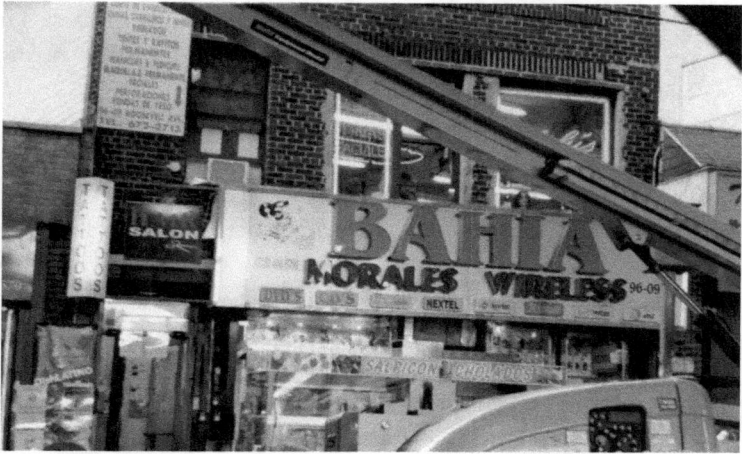

This is our apartment in Corona, Queens. The window on the left was my bedroom, which at the time had no glass on the top half.

The only time the room was uncomfortable was in the winter. I don't recall suffering with the summer heat in that room, but the winters were brutal. In addition to there being no heat source in the room, the one window in the room was broken. The top portion had been completely missing ever since we moved in, and my dad attempted to fix it, or at least cover it, by covering the hole with a piece of cardboard and taping it to the frame. He refused to pay to have the glass replaced. How much could that have cost? It didn't matter to him because the outside air was not going into the main apartment.

So for the next two to three years that we lived there, the outside air penetrated the cardboard and filled the room. There were many winter nights that were so cold in that room, I could see air smoke when I breathed. It was just as cold inside as it was outside. Even though I had a heater, it would only help for a short while because Dad, who had access to the electrical circuit box in the kitchen, would switch off the breaker to my room at night. He knew

I had the heater on, and it was costing him money. He never considered that had he fixed the window, the heater would not come on as frequently.

This was a constant battle, and one that led to many confrontations and arguments. Each time he turned it off, I ran into the kitchen to switch the circuit breaker on when the cold awakened me in the middle of the night. He didn't care that I was freezing. He was only concerned with how expensive the electric bill might be. That is how I lived in this room during my junior and senior years at Newtown High School, and my first year at Baruch College.

Nonetheless, that room was my refuge from the rest of the family. If I wanted to watch television, I had to go sit in the living room, but I seldom did that. Whenever I needed to use the bathroom, I sometimes ran back and forth between my room and the main living area to check its availability. If I didn't time it right, I lost out to someone else waiting because they were in the main area and easily saw when it became available sooner than I could.

Since I didn't eat Mom's cooking anymore, I never used the kitchen. My meals were usually outside at a diner on my way to school, or at a nearby fast-food restaurant, or at the Cuban restaurant, La Lechonera, at the corner of Junction Boulevard and Roosevelt Avenue, just steps from our apartment. There I could purchase a Cuban pork sandwich at a reasonable price. Some evenings I just sat in my room eating potato chips and drinking a soda for dinner.

Occasionally, I treated myself to dinner at the Cuban-Chinese restaurant on Junction Boulevard. There I could get fried pork chops Cuban style and fried rice, or rice and beans. When I found that place, it was the first time I realized that someone could speak both Chinese and Spanish. I stepped to the counter and asked for my meal in Spanish. The waiter behind the counter yelled the order to the kitchen—in Mandarin. I was so naïve, I found that hilarious.

After wandering around the parks and neighborhood for two or three weeks as a high school dropout, I quickly became bored. Being out of school and having no job gave me a taste of how empty that lifestyle could be and I didn't like it. Seeing my friends like Cheo doing things that I thought were destructive actually served as my motivation to return to school. I realized that dropping out to spite my parents wasn't accomplishing anything. They didn't see school as important, so I was only fooling and hurting myself.

The gym teacher calling me out for attending class for the first time in forty-five days played a role as well. Suddenly, I wanted to show him that I could be a successful student and a person to be proud of. I worried about what kind of career I might have without an education. I knew that I did not want to work at a Jack in the Box all my life. I remembered having a taste of how people with money lived when I was delivering groceries and meat in midtown Manhattan, and liked that lifestyle better.

I couldn't speak with my parents about my confusion, so I had to figure out my future for myself. I was at a crossroads, and felt that only I could determine if my destiny was going to be in the streets with gangs and menial jobs to make ends meet, and thus live a life similar to my parents', or if I was going to chart my own path to be better than that.

I made a decision that I wanted to be better, be successful, and elevate my standard of living. I also craved more space after years of living in cramped apartments with four brothers and sisters and Mom and Dad, always sharing one bathroom, with the five of us sleeping in one bedroom for most of my young life. I also had visions of being able to afford to live wherever, and however, I wanted. I yearned in my innermost self, in my guts, for total independence. I wanted to make sure I controlled my life and not let elements around me control it.

I have always been fortunate to have what I call "my living angels" to provide encouragement and open doors throughout my journey to a better life. Whether it was Russell, who gave me a job in his deli when I was twelve and taught me how to be responsible, or Mrs. Israel at PS 6 in the South Bronx, who showed me that an adult can care about me when she protected me from another teacher, or many others I have met throughout my life. I consider these people my living angels, who were there to encourage me, teach me, inspire me, and help me keep my dreams and aspirations alive and strong.

With a change of heart about dropping out of school and a yearning for a much better life, the second step was when I walked to Newtown High School and re-enrolled. That's when I learned that as a minor I needed one of my parents to sign me out of school, but not to re-enroll. I quickly resumed my junior year, missing only a few, but critical, weeks. My hours were from 8 a.m. to noon, which meant I could work earlier than the graveyard shift and have more time for schoolwork. Walking past the Jack in the Box on Junction Boulevard near 37th Avenue, I noticed that a former manager, Larry, who I worked for at the Astoria Boulevard location for a time, was now a manager there, so I stopped in to see him.

I wasn't sure that I could work at that company again because of my past friction with Ashraf, but Larry had been nice to me before and I thought I could at least say hello. I was hoping Larry would remember that he and I worked well together in the past and would give me an opportunity. He asked me how I was making ends meet. When I told him I wasn't working, he hired me despite the protest of Ron, the regional manager. This allowed me to get back on track, focus on school, and have a job that I enjoyed and knew how to do.

With the telephone line I paid to have installed in my room being the only phone in the home, I had to guard against someone at home breaking in to use the phone and run up my bill unbeknownst to me. My parents did not have a phone; whenever they did, it was inevitably cut for non-payment. I installed a padlock on my door for security. Sadly, respect for others was not high on the list of character traits at home.

One day I was coming home from school, and as I walked up the stairs, I noticed my dad unscrewing the hinge from the padlock to get into my room and use my telephone. I blew a gasket and argued with him to leave my stuff alone. I found out that either he or Mom or Nelson was sneaking into my room repeatedly to use the telephone or to steal money if I left any there. I tried to flatten the heads on the screws to keep my family from sneaking in, but that wasn't very successful. They were disrespectful and kept sneaking into my room, despite my protests. I tried to make sure not to have loose valuables in there that could disappear, but sometimes I would forget and let down my guard. My biggest risk was that they would run up my phone bill. At least that is what I thought.

Having returned to school, things were progressing pretty well for me. I completed my third year at Newtown with the help of some teachers, including Mr. Montesinos, my Spanish teacher, and Mrs. Cahill, my guidance counselor.

Mr. Montesinos was another angel who showed me patience and cooperation. At the time, I was not interested in learning Spanish, perhaps as a rebellion against my Puerto Rican parents speaking it at home and my desire to be different. I brought that rebellious attitude to Spanish class, but rather than scolding me or giving me a failing grade, Mr. Montesinos took a rather creative and constructive approach to dealing with me. He told me that he wanted me to participate in class, and that I could respond in English, if I preferred. He let me sit in the back of the room and read or draw, as long as I did not disrupt the class. He knew I liked drawing action heroes, and allowed me to do that if I did not want to participate in the class. Initially, I did sit in the back of the room and draw, but after some time I began participating and speaking Spanish.

As part of my renewed focus on a better future, and returning to school and working, I made a third decision that turned out to be the most painful. I broke up with Robin. My thinking at the time was that she wasn't focused on school and was about to drop out, and I was afraid that would interfere with my plans to finish school and go to college.

In retrospect, it was a drastic and selfish decision. I could have, and should have, counseled Robin to remain in school and follow a similar path to mine for the good of her future. There is no telling if she might have heeded my advice, but I should have tried. But having witnessed my parents remain in a destructive relationship, I vowed that if I had to make hard decisions to walk away from a relationship, I was going to do that without hesitation. Robin and I were close, and I was close to her mom, Helene, her sister, Andrea, and especially to her younger brother, Paul. I had become like a big brother to him, especially after his dad left. I did not even say good-bye to any of them, and that bothered me for a long time.

I attempted to get back together with Robin after a couple of weeks, but she was not interested. We saw each other a few times over the subsequent couple of years, but we never reunited. I don't know what became of Robin,

Andrea, and Helene, but I know that Paul became a lawyer in New York, which made me proud.

Newtown High School had an internship program where selected seniors had a chance to spend the first semester of their final year working in the business world as a way of getting real-world experience. Instead of going to classes that semester, the students in the program would go to work in an area of business that interested them. It was a way of preparing them for college and beyond. Some students did internships at radio stations if they aspired to be disc jockeys; hospitals if they wanted to be doctors or nurses. Some aspiring stock brokers were at Wall Street investment companies, and some who wanted to be lawyers were at law firms. One kid who wanted to be a television producer interned at The Children's Television Network, where *Sesame Street* was produced and broadcast.

I found another angel in a speech teacher in the English department who recommended me for the program. I mentioned that my aspiration was to go into business as an accountant, and my internship was confirmed at a midtown Manhattan advertising company that designed display ads for consumer products companies. I don't recall the name of the firm, and I don't know if it continues to exist, but I remember that the CEO was a man named Richard Leeds.

Thanks to that English teacher who got me into the internship program in my senior year at Newtown, I was working Monday to Friday in a midtown Manhattan office. It felt so different from my days when I was in the city delivering groceries and meat. I felt that I was on the inside now.

They didn't give me an official role or a specific function at the company, and I was floating among the various departments. I tended to gravitate to the art department, where the artists were responsible for creating the model ads and displays that were sent out for mass production, after the clients approved them.

I also enjoyed spending time with the sales department because the sales guys were polished and always wore suits. I liked the creative aspect of the art department and the business acumen of the sales guys. I thoroughly enjoyed seeing firsthand how the business world functioned; how the products were created and sold. That's what I realized that I enjoyed! It wasn't accounting that excited me.

One day I found myself in the elevator with a couple of sales guys as we headed out to lunch. They asked me what I wanted to do with my future. My response was that I wanted to make lots of money. When one of the guys asked me what a lot of money was, I thought for a moment and responded, "Forty thousand dollars." That was in 1974 dollars, of course. I had no idea if they thought it was a lot of money, but I had to answer with something. None of them responded or gave me an idea of how much money they were making at the time, which was what I really wanted to know.

Bill Silver, who was probably the top salesman at the firm, invited me to a customer lunch at a fancy restaurant near the office. La Scala may no longer exist today, but it was quite an impressive restaurant for me, a seventeen-year-old high school intern. I did not have a jacket, so the restaurant provided me one. All the tables were covered with white linen. The restaurant was in a brownstone building on a side street, and we had to walk down a few steps to get inside. I had no idea what to order, so I ordered the roast beef, which was a huge chunk of meat. I asked for an end cut because I prefer my meat cooked medium well. It was too large to finish, and I only ate a small portion and left the rest. I must have weighed in the neighborhood of 135 pounds, and I could not possibly eat all of that meat. But it was delicious!

It was nice of Bill to invite me to my first business lunch. It was a pleasant experience. I went from delivering meat at places like La Scala, to dining there as a customer. That was pretty cool, I thought. Yet, the people I was having lunch with had no idea that I lived in a room with a missing window, no heat, and was sleeping wearing a coat in the winter to stay as warm as possible. How ironic! The internship opened my eyes to two important realizations about myself: I enjoyed the creative aspect of business and the entrepreneurial side; and I did not enjoy the back office part that accounting represented. With that knowledge I had to figure out what I wanted to do for a career as I prepared for college.

Chapter Seventeen

That year, preparing for graduation was an adventure. I was so depressed that my parents didn't have any idea I was graduating, I didn't even purchase a graduation ring, attend the prom, or go to any graduation ceremonies. For these reasons, and more, graduation from high school was not a happy experience for me. There was no celebration!

I remembered that Mom and Dad didn't attend my junior high school graduation, so I wasn't expecting them to attend, or help me plan for, my high school graduation. I was correct. Nelson had stolen my JHS graduation ring, and that discouraged me from buying a high school version.

I was also perplexed by the process of college applications, but could not talk to anyone at home to overcome my confusion. I didn't know how to apply, which schools were best for me, or how to focus on a curriculum. Visiting any school before applying was not something I thought was possible. The guidance counselor, Mrs. Cahill, helped me, but she was also busy helping many other students. I applied to, and was accepted by, Baruch College of the City University of New York. I probably would have preferred to apply to other schools, but I was not at all prepared financially or otherwise to consider other options.

Before I could attend Baruch in the fall of 1975, I had to graduate from high school. I was short a few credits, due to my truancy the prior year, so I had to go to summer school. I accepted that as the price I had to pay for missing so much school the prior year, and I was determined to complete the two classes I had to take that summer. I considered it a welcome challenge and enthusiastically embraced it.

I remember that the summer was very hot in July and August, and the classrooms at Jamaica High School, where I attended summer school, were hot and sticky. Those old public school buildings had no air-conditioning, so the teacher kept the windows open to let in whatever breeze was blowing. I was happy to be there because I was determined to graduate on time and attend college in the fall. I aced the classes, which made the rest of my summer a happy one.

That same summer, I proudly purchased my first car—a used Ford LTD, a huge old car, but it was mine. It cost me $400 in cash. I got the car registered, proudly screwed my plates on, and bought some air fresheners to hang on the rearview mirror. Mom wanted me to place stickers on the back of the car along with a Puerto Rican flag, but I refused. I wasn't into advertising anything on my car. I was more concerned with making sure it didn't get stolen as it sat parked at night in Corona, Queens. I got up as early as 7 a.m. to check on it, and washed and waxed it often to keep it sparkling.

Unfortunately, that car lasted me only two months. I junked it after nearly killing myself. I was visiting Robin in the Bronx one Sunday and left her apartment in the evening. As I headed toward the Bronx River Parkway, I was unable to stop at a red light when my brakes failed. I quickly made a U-turn just before getting on the Parkway and headed back toward Robin's home, looking out for streets with no traffic. I continued to pump the brakes, but they failed to respond. I tried to find streets that were uphill to reduce my speed and soon found my way back onto Robin's block, which was empty of traffic and was slightly uphill.

I purposely crashed the car into the wrought-iron fence of a school directly across the street from Robin's apartment building and finally brought the car to a stop. Amazingly, the school's fence was not damaged. I took the subway home. The next day I called a nearby service station to tow the car to their shop and check it out for me. I thought I might be able to sell it for a couple hundred dollars to the service station. I was sure they were capable of repairing it and could keep it or sell it for a profit. I was disappointed when the owner of the station offered me twenty-five dollars, net of the towing and service charges. I thought he took advantage of the situation, and of me, but, as we both knew, I didn't have much of a choice. He had the leverage and I had none. I sold him the car, picked up the money, and went back home.

Riding the subway, especially late at night, was always risky and I thought my car was the antidote I needed. With my car gone, I was back to traveling through the city by train, sometimes risking my life. My usual route was to take the number 7 train to Times Square, then the number 2 train to Pelham Parkway or Allerton Avenue.

One late night, maybe around midnight, I boarded the number 2 train at Pelham Parkway to head back home. There was a group of about twenty black guys and one police officer, who was also black. The group was arguing with the police officer and threatening to shoot him. It was stuff that we often heard of on the television news or read of in newspapers.

It was a scary scene for me to know that some of the guys were, according to what they were saying, carrying guns and I was sitting nearby. They kept harassing the police officer, telling him that he had better get off at the next stop or they would shoot him. It was incredible that two stops later the officer got off the train while the guys were yelling at him. They didn't bother any of the other passengers in the car, but the police officer was understandably afraid for his own life and he didn't consider that the gang might hurt other passengers. He didn't call for backup and have an army of officers meet the train at the next stop. I was relieved when the gang got off the train at the following stop.

It was a scene that could have easily turned much worse. What if the police officer reacted differently and pulled his gun out of its holster to confront the guys who threatened to shoot him, instead of getting off the train? It might have turned into a shootout, with one or more of the guys shot by the officer, and possibly the officer himself shot by one in the gang. That scenario could have easily resulted in other passengers being injured or killed. Who knows, perhaps that police officer did the right thing to diffuse the confrontation by walking away.

I don't know what the gang ultimately did that night. Did they get off the train and rob someone or a store, at gunpoint? Did they go on a killing spree that we never heard of or read about? If that was a risk, then the police officer, to protect the public, should have called for backup and had a large force of police officers meet the train at the next stop. He would be protecting himself as well as the public at large. Who knows, he might have done that and I just didn't witness it.

On another trip, I saw a familiar guy from Robin's neighborhood riding the number 2 train while we headed to the Bronx. He was a guy who I knew was attracted to her, and so he didn't care much for me. The next day Robin, almost in tears, told me that he told her he saw me on the train and was thinking of shooting me with the gun he was carrying. I don't know if he was bluffing to impress a girl or if he was serious, but Robin was concerned enough to warn me to be careful on the trains.

I was always lucky to have my angels in heaven keep me from serious harm. Whatever harm came my way was a lesson for me to learn from. Ever since I had an encounter with some punks in East Elmhurst, I carried a large knife, except when I went to school.

One evening Robin and I were hanging out in the lobby of an apartment building on Allerton Avenue, when a large group of gang members entered the building. They were followed by about ten police officers. There was tremendous commotion and confusion as the police officers were questioning the gang members and frisking them.

Robin and I were sitting in a section of the building that was about thirty feet from the entrance and around a corner, so we were somewhat hidden when a police officer approached and questioned us. I was afraid because I was carrying my knife. I thought that if the officer frisked me, I was definitely going to be in trouble.

Suddenly, standing in front of us, he told us that since we were not with that group, we should leave the building. As soon as he turned around to walk away, I quietly reached into my pocket, pulled the knife out, stooped down quickly, and set it down on the floor against a wall. I was careful not to let the knife knock the ground so it did not make a noise that might have caused the police officer to turn around. Robin and I quickly walked out of the building and left the scene. I wonder if the police officer found the knife and blamed its presence on the gang members.

My lesson there was clear: Stop carrying a knife. My angels took that knife away from me by having me place it on that floor—before it got me into serious trouble.

The car troubles I'd had made me think that my next car would have to be a brand-new one. The Ford LTD had left me stranded on the Queensboro Bridge once, before the incident with the failing brakes, and I had no confidence in used cars. But, for the time being, I was focused on starting college and working at Jack in the Box to pay for school and support myself. A new car was a dream for a future time.

At Baruch I began by taking twelve credits my first semester and working an average of forty to fifty hours per week. It was a busy schedule, so I didn't have time to hang out much, which was a good thing. My busy schedule certainly kept me out of trouble.

My parents, even though we lived in the same apartment, never asked me anything about college. They were simply upset that I chose that path, and that I wasn't working to support them. All the money I earned was used for tuition, books, transportation, and meals. I had to stop giving my mother part of my pay in order to meet my expenses. I thought that my parents should be happy that I was studying to advance myself, and it wasn't costing them any money. But that was not the case.

In the years I worked at Jack in the Box, I never witnessed a robbery until one Monday evening in 1975. There were only two of us working at the restaurant. I was at the grill preparing an egg sandwich for a customer, and there was a young lady working the register. The guy who ordered the sandwich was the only customer. The evenings during the beginning of the week were usually quiet with very few customers.

The person who was there, in retrospect, ordered something that he knew drove me out of the way, as I had to go back to the grill, leaving the cashier alone. Although I was only perhaps ten feet away, it was plenty of distance for him to do some damage. The cashier rang his order on the cash register. When the register opened, the man leaped over the counter and grabbed as much money as he could. The cashier was stunned, of course, and screamed.

I saw the man pulling back from the register with dollar bills in his hand. Realizing what had happened, my immediate reaction was to grab a knife to protect my coworker and myself. When the man ran out of the store, I ran outside with the knife in my hand. Enough time (minutes) had elapsed for me to realize that I could not catch up to him and that it was not a good idea anyway. I was absolutely astonished that someone would steal from me. I took it quite personally. I was able to get a good look at the man from behind the grill area, as I leaned below the warming light area of the food trays, to see what was going on when the cashier screamed. I knew I could easily identify him if I saw him again.

After running some ten feet outside with a knife, I thought it was best not to go after the guy. I went back into the restaurant and called the police, and then my manager. We filed the police report, and I thought that would be the end of it. About two weeks later, the same guy came back into the restaurant. Recognizing him, I told my manager, who was in the office upstairs, and he immediately called the police. The police arrived within five minutes, and with the guy still in the restaurant, presumably waiting for his food order, they arrested him. They cuffed him and brought him to the upstairs office for me to identify him. My instant reaction was "Oh, oh, this guy now knows what I look like." The guy pleaded with me to tell them he wasn't the guy they were looking for, but he definitely was. I had no choice but to tell the police the truth. Now he knew that I was the person who identified him to the police, which I was not happy about. We both lived in the same neighborhood, and I was afraid he would have his friends attack me while I walked outside.

After a few days I got a call to appear before a grand jury to tell my story to see if there was sufficient evidence to have him indicted. I was hesitant, fearful of retaliation by his friends. It seemed much too close to home. I spoke to Ron and he assured me that he would accompany me to court.

Ron was 6'7", so I felt more comfortable that he was going to be with me through the process. I had no idea what a grand jury was or how the court system worked. The details I presented were sufficient to get an indictment. Then it got more interesting.

Once I got a subpoena to appear at the trial, I was on my own. Ron was no longer interested in going with me to court. I felt he deceived me by assuring me he would go with me when he knew he would only do that until I was under subpoena.

The defendant attempted to intimidate me by having a group of his unsavory-looking friends in court during the trial. It was a stressful and frightening experience for me. Outside of the trial, guys showed up at my job to continue their intimidation tactics. They stopped at the drive-thru, and when one of us answered, they sent messages asking me not to go to court. One afternoon I was in my assistant manager's car as we drove to another restaurant to pick up supplies (we typically traded supplies among the stores in the region), and we were followed by a group of guys.

Since I was under subpoena, I had no choice but to go to the trial, which lasted only two or three appearances. At the end of the trial, the prosecutor informed me that the defendant was likely to go to jail for two or three years, and that I would be living somewhere else when he got out. That gave me more motivation to get out of Corona as soon as possible.

That frightening experience left me feeling disappointed because I felt that Ron betrayed me when he refused to go with me to the trial. I knew it was the right thing to do because I never wanted anyone to get away with doing harm to others. The guy stole from us and needed to be held accountable. I also felt, however, that the company was responsible for providing better support to me. My parents had no idea about this event, from the robbery, to the court trial, and especially about my fears through the ordeal. I didn't want to scare Mom by telling her the details.

At home I had to deal with Nelson's misdeeds. One day I received a notice from the Parking Violations Bureau of New York informing me that I had a number of unpaid violations, and they threatened to suspend my license. I was surprised because I had never gotten as much as a parking ticket. As I looked further into the matter, it occurred to me that Nelson had stolen my driver's license and was driving around the city accumulating summonses in my name. I remembered that I discovered I was missing part of my driver's license from my room.

When I approached him about it, Nelson matter-of-factly admitted having gotten the summonses with my license and handed me what was actually the renewal portion of my driver's license. Back then a New York State driver's license was in two parts and did not include a photo.

Nelson went with me to the Parking Violations Bureau and paid all the summonses, about $300 worth, including penalties. It was not exactly costly for him since he gathered the money from girlfriends. I did find it suspicious that he turned over to me the stolen document so easily and, just as easily, went to the PVB with me and paid the fines, but I was happy to have my driving record untarnished. It was vital to me to have my license in good standing.

Unfortunately, Nelson developed into a petty criminal. He was irresponsible, conniving, and unscrupulous. I used to tell Mom that it was her fault he grew up that way. She reinforced his unrighteous behavior by not correcting him with proper discipline. I believe he inherited a weak character that made it easy for him to go down the wrong path in life, especially if not tugged with guidance along the right path. As we got older I actually stopped speaking with him, even when we lived in the same apartment with my parents. On the street, I avoided acknowledging him when I saw him. He represented everything I didn't like. My parents succeeded in making him a burden to the world rather than shaping him to become a productive member of society. Our relationship as brothers started out as love, then over the years developed into sadness, and ultimately all of that gave way to overwhelming anger.

Upon reflection I have come to regret that I did not do something to give him the guidance and direction my parents could not. I just did not have the maturity to do that. I allowed his transgressions against me to stoke my anger.

When we were young boys of maybe eight and ten years old, we played and explored as all brothers do. We had a love for each other and naturally protected one another. That eventually changed. As we got older and I saw firsthand the transgressions Nelson was committing, it was sad for me to see that he was heading down a path that would lead to no good—and it seemed there was nothing I could do to change him. I was sad for him and angry with my parents. They did nothing to hold him accountable early in life in order to keep him from becoming a miscreant. Once he started stealing from me, I became so angry with him that I could not believe he was my brother. I didn't want to be his brother. I wanted nothing to do with him. That makes me sad, especially now that he is no longer with us.

I recall standing on the subway platform one afternoon and seeing him walk by. I didn't even say hello to him. I believed, and often repeated this to my parents, that if a person is wrong, regardless of who he is, he has to pay the consequences for his actions, and should not be excused or forgiven just because of family ties. That was too harsh!

The frequent arguments with my parents about this were fruitless. They protected Nelson, especially Mom, even though he was wrong in committing criminal or unethical acts against his own family members. My argument to them was that if I had a brother who committed a crime, I considered him a criminal. The fact that he was my brother did not make him less of a criminal. Had he been caught by the police and hauled into a court room, I am sure that the judge was not going to say, "Oh, you are Nelson, son of Victoria Vicente and brother of Israel Vicente. Then you are free to go and your crime is forgiven." No, I am sure that would not happen. Nelson had to pay for the consequences of his actions, like everyone else must. I tried to tell my parents many times that he needed help and discipline; otherwise he was eventually going to end up in serious trouble.

Mom's point of view was that he was my brother and should be forgiven. I have never agreed with that logic and found it ridiculous. He had done to me many things that were wrong, and I resented that my parents never held him accountable. It was their poor excuse for letting him do as he pleased, and it created a criminal, sad as that is.

One evening I came home to see that someone had broken into my room again. The telltale signs were the loose hinges to the padlock on the door. Someone didn't have time to fully screw them back in when they heard me coming up the stairs. By the time I scaled the fourteen steps leading to my room on one side and the rest of the house on the other side, the hallway was empty.

I was so upset at seeing the evidence of tampering with the lock that I ran into the living room and began yelling at my parents, asking who was in my room. Everyone denied it, so I kept yelling and warning them to stay out. (I should have done a better job padlocking the door.)

Dad stood up from the couch and made a motion to strike me. I pushed him down on the couch and warned him that if he ever hit me again, I would hit him right back. He was so scared that I could see the whites of his eyes. He never attempted to hit me again.

Nelson was there as well, and I started yelling at him. Suspecting it was Nelson who was either in my room or about to go in, I went to grab him and threaten him, when he grabbed a kitchen knife and tried to stab me. He didn't harm me, but it was enough to diffuse the confrontation. I went back to my room to calm down and check my belongings to see if anything was missing.

My parents had raised us with a mentality of being takers rather than givers. Recently, I was watching Joel Osteen on television. He was speaking about four types of people that he equated to a story told to him by a pilot friend, who explained the four main attributes of a plane: lift, thrust, weight, and drag. Osteen, in this speech, said that it is similar with people. We will meet some who will be lifters, helping to lift us to higher achievements; thrusters who will propel us forward in life; those who will try to burden us with their weight, making it difficult for us to move forward and upward; and those who will want to drag us down with them.

This struck a chord with me because growing up, and as I got old enough to think for myself, I felt that my parents, unfortunately, were living in constant negativity, always feeling sorry for themselves and expecting others to bail them out of one situation after another. They, in turn, were rarely willing to do anything to help anyone unless there was some gain for them. Thinking about it in terms of Joel Osteen's analogy, they were dragging their burdens with heavy weight, and were teaching us to be that way as well.

They were perfectly fine if their kids wound up being like them, and perhaps that is why they favored Nelson and protected him. Even though he grew to steal from his own brother, drive a car without a license, and drop out of high school and not work, they always made excuses for him in order to protect him, rather than help him become a better person. Mom often scolded me for yelling at Nelson after I discovered that he had stolen things from my room. She never confronted him or lectured him in order to teach him to be a better person and a respectful brother. It was frustrating and incomprehensible to me that I was made to be the bad person for yelling at him and wanting to hold him accountable.

The absolute worst case, and perhaps the most serious example of his criminal behavior, was when I pressed criminal charges on Nelson for fraudulently using my driver's license again. The second time! My sophomore year in college I had saved enough money to purchase a brand-new car, a 1976 burgundy Camaro with a white vinyl top. I absolutely loved that car.

One Friday evening, Wil and I were driving to the campus of Stony Brook University on Long Island to visit a girlfriend of his. On campus we apparently went through a stop sign that I didn't see, and were stopped by the campus police. After they checked their computer, they told me that my license was suspended for failure to pay some moving violations summonses. I told the officer that I was sure there must be some mistake because I had never gotten so much as a parking ticket, much less a moving violation citation. He checked again and assured me that my license was indeed suspended, and that he would have to confiscate my car since I was driving illegally.

I pleaded with him that we lived far away and didn't have a way to get back home. After listening to my desperate pleas, he let me keep my car, but gave me a summons and we were able to leave. As I put together the pieces, it occurred to me that Nelson must have accumulated the summonses in my name after he had stolen my driver's license the first time; it was only logical that he would do it again. I was puzzled, though, because he had returned the stolen part of my license after the first offense. So, how could he have done it again?

It turns out he was so cynical and sinister that before he returned my stolen driver's license, he created a duplicate. He maliciously and irresponsibly drove around the city accumulating more than ten speeding tickets and other moving violations, without regard for the damage he was causing to my driving record. On top of which, he did not pay any of the summonses, causing the suspension of my license.

The following Monday morning, I traveled on the subway to the DMV in Jamaica, Queens, to get a list of the summonses on my record. I needed the details and the amount owed in my name. I took that information and confronted Nelson in front of Mom. Astonishingly, he admitted that he had been the one to get those summonses. I wanted him to take responsibility for his misdeeds by paying the fines and restoring my good driving record. That was the immediate priority. Longer term, I wondered how in the world I was going to get him to never do this again. What was it going to take?

I went to the DMVs in the Bronx and Long Island and learned they required a letter from me explaining the details of my case. I opened a case with the DMV Field Investigation Unit and in my letter, I explained that my half-brother had fraudulently used my driving identification and was the one who was issued the summonses. They wrote back stating that in order for them to open a case, I had to file criminal charges against my brother.

Chapter Eighteen

I was more than willing to file criminal charges and hold Nelson accountable for his illegal and harmful actions. I thought that since this was the second time he had used my driving identification illegally, he was not going to learn a lesson by simply paying the summonses. We had already been down that road. But perhaps the best way to teach him a lesson was to have him put in jail. I was very willing to do that. I filed criminal charges and had to serve him the summons to appear in court.

One evening, I found out that he was at Aunt Irma and Uncle Laddy's apartment. I went there and served him the papers and told him, "I will see you in court." Irma and Laddy were appalled that I did such a thing as to try to have my *own brother* put in jail. But that didn't matter to me. I wanted to be left alone. Neither they, nor my parents, considered the magnitude of the problem he had created for me.

I found it ridiculous and cynical that at our first court date, as we waited outside the courtroom in Kew Gardens, Queens, to have my case called, Nelson turned to me and said that I should be ashamed of what I was doing to our mom by bringing him to court, and that I was making her suffer. This was the mentality being permeated in that household. My family could do anything they wanted, even if it was illegal, as long as it was for their benefit, and regardless of what harm they caused to others. And they should bear no repercussions. I told Nelson I didn't care and would not stop until he wound up in jail.

Throughout the ordeal of the two offenses, not once did he apologize. He showed no remorse whatsoever.

I appeared in court wearing a suit and tie and carrying a briefcase. When we were called before the judge, he asked if I was Nelson's attorney. I thought that was ironic. The judge told Nelson he needed to get an attorney and re-scheduled the case for a later date. The next time we appeared in court, Nelson did not have an attorney present. The judge was furious with him and told him if he did not appear the next time with an attorney, he was going to lock him up.

After that court appearance, frightened by the judge's stern promise, Nelson flew down to Puerto Rico to hide at the home of one of my mother's aunts in the town of Guayama. He never showed up in court again. I won the case and my driving record was restored, all blemishes removed. I believe that my determination to take him to court and not succumb to pressure by other family members made him stop using my name as a driver. He realized I was serious about taking him to court and wanting him locked up.

That unfortunate episode with Nelson took my time away from school, so it was absolutely an unnecessary distraction. Once it was over, I was able to return my full concentration to my two primary activities, college and work.

My freshman year at Baruch, during the early part of my second semester, I became ill with mononucleosis. The fatigue from working forty to fifty hours each week, along with a full load of classes, took its toll. I was staying up to study and do homework late into the night. There were many nights that I got home from work around midnight and stayed up until 5 a.m. to study, eventually falling asleep for a few hours before getting ready for school. My poor diet of potato chips, Cokes or Colt 45, and fast food certainly didn't help either.

People used to tell me that mononucleosis was a kissing disease, but I didn't have a girlfriend during this time, as I was too busy. I suppose I could have made time for a relationship, but I wasn't interested. I wanted to focus on school without the added distraction.

I remember that I had gone to visit Vivian, a friend in East Elmhurst. I found out that she was in the same high school internship program I had been in. We had first met when she attended Catholic school at St. Gabriel on Astoria Boulevard in East Elmhurst with my brother, Wil, and sister, Evelyn. She might have been twelve when we first met. I was fourteen. I liked her long, curly black hair surrounding her smooth brown complexion. Fast-forward some years and she was seventeen when by happenstance we reconnected and she invited me to her home. She introduced me to her family before we settled in her room to chat. I felt fine that evening, not a clue that I was getting sick.

The next evening, Vivian called me at home, but I could not so much as speak a word to her. I was in so much pain, with sores throughout my entire mouth, that words would not come out. In that pre-texting era, I could not communicate with Vivian, and it felt horrible because she had no idea what was wrong. Mom took me to the Elmhurst hospital emergency room, where they prescribed some medication to numb the pain, but it didn't really help. I was sick in bed for eight consecutive days and lost nearly twenty pounds during that time. All I could do was drink milkshakes through a straw by pushing the straw to the back of my mouth and swallowing slowly. If the straw touched any part of my mouth except the very back near my throat, I screamed in pain. It was excruciating!

When I healed, I went back to school, but had to drop my French class. I had lost so much time that I found it difficult to catch up. I had not worked during this time either and had very little money to travel on the subway to and from school, and I was concerned about that as well.

One afternoon while I was in school, I got hungry and went to the diner on 23rd Street near Park Avenue. I sat at the counter and ordered a cup of hot tea and a toasted bagel with butter. My hunger prevailed that afternoon and I forgot I had no money to pay for the subway to get back home. Or maybe I knew that, but my primary need at that moment was to satiate my hunger. All I could do was ask the token booth clerk to please let me through the turnstile and I would pay him the next day. That was my plan as I approached the 23rd Street station.

When I got downstairs to the subway station, I saw a transit police officer and adjusted my plan. I decided to explain that I went to school down the street at Baruch and had no money for the token to get back home. He didn't speak much, but he was nice enough to let me through, and I was able to get back home.

I was grateful that I found a nice police officer who understood my situation. Come to think of it, I have come in contact with many wonderful and compassionate police officers over the years. Another time was when two officers saw me walking home late at night from Jack in the Box along Astoria Boulevard and stopped to give me a lift home in their patrol car.

I didn't feel I could ask my parents for money to go to school, so I had to quickly get back to work. I had some money in the bank but it was being quickly depleted, and I was concerned about running completely out. After a brief search, I was able to get a job at the Wall Street law firm of Davis Polk & Wardwell, assisting with office maintenance.

The office manager was a nice older man who allowed me to work flexible hours based on my school schedule.

That job was in a beautiful office building, One Chase Plaza, a short walking distance from the World Trade Centers. I think our offices were on the forty-first floor, with a great view of the East River on one side and the financial district on the other, with the Twin Towers in clear view. They also had a great cafeteria that was subsidized by the firm, so the prices were reasonable and ideal for a student like me.

I worked with an older Ukrainian man named Boris, who was the lead maintenance man, doing everything from hanging pictures for the attorneys, putting furniture together, moving furniture around the office, and repairing anything that needed repair. He took a liking to me and took me under his wing to teach me his craft.

Boris knew that I was in college, and many times when I arrived at the office after school in the afternoon, he had food from the cafeteria for me in our maintenance room (a converted storage closet). The kitchen staff often gave him hot food and slices of pie, and he made sure he shared with me. I always appreciated that, and I helped him with his work in return. Whatever he needed, I was eager to help.

It was at Davis Polk & Wardwell that I got my hands-on introduction to computers. Although I was taking a FORTRAN programming course at Baruch, the students didn't have a direct way of coding on the computer. We were instructed to write the code on pre-printed, formatted sheets and hand them to the professor. He then had to input the code after class and give us the printed code compilation at the next class, complete with errors, explaining why the program failed to compile. It wasn't the most efficient way of getting the coding done and fixed, so it took a long time to get a successful compile.

At Davis Polk & Wardwell, they were installing a new computer during the summer of 1976 and hired a few college students to do the data entry. They asked me if I wanted to be a part of that team, thanks to the office manager who liked me and wanted to give me a chance to do things other than office maintenance. I remember seeing that as an opportunity to learn something new and said yes. The project was to automate all the legal records accumulated by attorneys. I spent that summer doing data entry full time. I had a hunch that it was an experience I would be able to leverage later on. I knew that computer automation in corporations and government was the new buzz. I certainly didn't know how big it was going to become. Maybe no one did. But I was on the ground floor of a new industry. Fast-forward some thirty years and I was fortunate to become CEO of my very own software company—thanks to that initial opportunity at Davis Polk that helped build my technical foundation.

The other kids on the team were nice and seemed smart. They were from different colleges like Pace University and NYU.

I completed my freshman year at Baruch with a B+ average, which I was happy with, considering I was juggling school and a full-time job.

All the while my parents were grumbling that I was a hotshot because I was going to college. It was something they never expected, or wanted. I felt that they were disappointed in me. As far as I was concerned, I was doing the best thing possible to improve my future. I believe that if my parents had embraced my aspirations to grow and improve—and had supported me—I would have had an easier time adjusting to the confusing life of college and would have enjoyed sharing all my experiences with them. I wish I could have shared all my future successes with them. The fact that they were not supportive and were always critical of my decision to go to college made me resent them.

I stopped working at Davis Polk & Wardwell during the fall semester of 1976, which was the start of my sophomore year. My decision to leave and the manner in which I left were both things I regretted. The people there were very good to me, and I made a bad decision in leaving.

I responded to an advertisement for a job near the Baruch campus that piqued my interest. The ad promised high income for just a few hours of work a day. I figured that if I could work fewer hours and make more money, why not? I was equally motivated by the prospect of working close to school. There was less travel time, less travel fare, and the same convenient hours as I had presently. At least that was my rationale. I interviewed for the position and was offered the job after they had me read from a script.

I had been improving my spoken English, working to eliminate the street slang I had picked up over the years in the Bronx and Queens. I taught myself to speak more clearly and pronounce words completely. I purchased a secondhand tape recorder, which I used to record myself reading school textbooks in my room late at night. I then replayed the recordings to critique my speech. I repeated this process, modifying the recording until it sounded like perfect English to me, or at least until I could no longer detect my street slang. I actually began this practice in my senior year of high school, as part of taking a speech class focused on public speaking.

The interviewer liked the way I read and offered me the job, a telemarketing position selling home cleaning products to homeowners, from a call list they provided. The only catch was that they required I start immediately, that afternoon. I thought that was odd, and told them I had another job I had to resign from first. They pressured me to quit right away because they needed me to start.

I felt the pressure and was afraid of losing the opportunity, so I called the office manager at the law firm to quit. I will never forget what he said to me when I told him I was quitting on the spot because the new job required that I start immediately. He said, "If they want you to quit your job on the spot without any notice, it is not a good job." He wished me luck and we hung up.

I felt a knot in my stomach and sensed that I had just made a bad decision. Sure enough, the job lasted two weeks and they fired me for not selling anything. I didn't like the job or the people, and I didn't believe in the products. I thought it was odd that anyone would buy the stuff over the phone. I know I wouldn't. The lesson was that if it sounds too good to be true, it is.

Chapter Nineteen

After that setback, I found a part-time job as an office clerk at an Italian steel importing company, Siderius, Inc., located in midtown on Avenue of the Americas. My job was running errands and helping with whatever the office needed.

If you believe, as I do, that everything happens for a reason, this job was another manifestation of that notion. If I had not made the poor decision to take on that telemarketing job, I might not have left Davis Polk & Wardwell. While I didn't know it at the time, I was destined to make that move and also get fired from the telemarketing job. It is what led me to find this job at Siderius, Inc. What I thought at the time was a bad decision turned into a great opportunity. Sometimes a door closes simply to open another door to lead you to greater favor.

After a few months on the job, I learned that Siderius had taken on a project to add a new computer system. They hired Steve Clayton, a recent college graduate from Texas who was related to the president of the company, to manage that project.

One day, out of curiosity, I walked into the conference room where two men were setting up the new system. I had a feeling that the new computer system was an opportunity for me to move up from an office clerk to a higher, better paying position. Steve was there with the consultant they hired to program and implement the software, a man named Joe Cather who was recommended by IBM, the hardware provider of the System 32 computer.

Encouraged by the confidence of a track record from Davis Polk, I casually mentioned to them that I had experience with computers, leveraging the data entry work I had done at the law firm. Steve didn't seem to have much prior experience with computers, so the timing was right. He wanted to be the manager and taskmaster, but he needed someone to be part of his team. He needed the person to do the data entry, run the reports, interact with Joe Cather, and reconcile discrepancies when they inevitably appeared. He could then focus on higher level management matters. The opportunity crystalized further when Joe took a liking to me, perhaps seeing in me a younger version of himself twenty years prior. My angels lined up the stars once again and presented me with a hand-in-glove opportunity.

Steve Clayton hired me on a part-time basis to do data entry on the new computer system until I transitioned out of my office clerk role. Luckily for me, Joe was nice enough to take me under his wing and coach me on the use of the computer. He turned out to be an incredibly positive influence on me. Years later when I worked as a project manager at Cushman and Wakefield, I hired Joe as a consultant for a brief project for which we needed outside help.

Even though things were going well for me at Baruch, and I was contently working and making money, I felt alone and depressed. Something was missing from my life. It was disheartening not having a family to share my experiences with. Except for the interactions with people at school or at work, I didn't socialize with anyone. I started to wonder what the purpose of my life was. I was eighteen, almost nineteen years old, and as I grew older my inner desire for a stable, loving family grew stronger.

I began reading books on philosophy, especially on existentialism. The one theme that made the most sense to me was the belief that an individual person was responsible for creating his or her own values and determining the meaning of his or her own life. It became important to me as I struggled with the confusion around the purpose of my life. My readings encouraged me to accept the fact that if I was going to have that loving family I craved, I would have to go about creating it for myself. In fact, it further validated my belief that whatever I wanted to achieve, I was fully responsible for.

We grew up Catholic and Mom took us to church pretty regularly when we were young, which in later years I thought was ironic given our chaotic home life. I also went to religious instruction in the Bronx after school a couple days a week, although my parents never had me perform my first Communion.

The experiences that drove me away from religion included all the bad things that my parents did while alleging to be religious. I saw their behavior and their actions in direct conflict with their professed belief in God and his holy son, Jesus. All the violence around our home didn't make sense for a family that believed in God. I found enough contradiction within the Gospels themselves without the added conflict at home.

Mom's interpretation of God grew more unbelievable to me over time. She often reminded us that God either rewarded us for a good deed or punished us for a bad deed. She often claimed to be a good Catholic, but beat me mercilessly for making a mistake. She claimed to be a good Catholic, but could cowardly abandon my dad and take us all away from him. If I didn't give her more money when I was working, she told me I was too materialistic and God was going to punish me for it.

One fall I purchased a suede jacket at a store in Manhattan, Wilson's Leather and Suede. The store didn't have my size, so they had to order the jacket. When I went to pick it up on the day they promised to have it, they said it had not yet arrived. This happened multiple times over several weeks and I was upset, thinking they had taken my money and would never produce the jacket. I mentioned my frustration and annoyance to my parents. Dad didn't care and said nothing. Mom reminded me that it was God's punishment because I was selfish. She figured that I should be unselfish and give her whatever money I had instead of buying the suede jacket. Eventually, Wilson's produced the jacket, so I guess God decided to lighten up on me.

All of these experiences helped to develop my attitude that I could only believe in what I could see, touch, and control. I developed a sense that I had to create my own future, and only I could control my life. I was learning to make my own "luck," just like I did by seeking out the opportunity to work on the new Siderius computer system. All the mistakes I was making as I grew older were contributing factors in my development. I remained cognizant of my mistakes, and analyzed them so as to avoid repeating them. At least that was my goal.

Consequently, all these events drove me away from religion. I could not understand the purpose of having faith or believing in a God that I could not see. Furthermore, if I thought of God as our ultimate protector, as Mom thought of him, then why would he let children be so mistreated the way we were by our parents? I could not rationalize that, so I didn't want any part of religion. I always felt that the priests were mere men and nuns mere women. There was nothing divine about them. As I got older and the many revelations of priests abusing children came to light, it further solidified my impression of them as mere humans committing unfathomable (and unforgivable) sins.

I was angry at my parents and everything they believed in, including God and the Catholic Church, which I saw as a business run by men who were there to trade their sermons in exchange for donations by the public. I preferred to be self-sufficient, and that is how I was growing up to be. I thought my dad was lazy and had no vision or aspirations, and I wanted to be different from him. I wanted to learn, grow, and work hard, to reach a socioeconomic level that would allow me to be free. I did not want to rely on anyone for food or shelter, not my parents and not the government, as my parents had to do at various times throughout our lives. The problem with that type of public assistance is that it can become a crutch; something expected and easy to become dependent on.

My sophomore year at Baruch was itself confusing as I struggled to figure out what I was going to do with my life, what I was going to become. I vacillated between confusion and fear. Would I succeed at Baruch? What was the point of going to college, especially since no one at home cared? When would I have enough money to truly, finally be on my own? Amidst my internal struggles, I continued forward at school.

I was very involved in school groups, and I sought to stay busy and learn as much as possible. Following up on the psychology class I took during my freshman year, I joined a group managed by that department to become a peer counselor to other students. It was a bit strange because it put me in an authority position where I had to counsel other students on how to adapt to college life. As a peer counselor, my role was to help the students deal with any issues they might have. Imagine, a young person as confused as I was helping other students who were just as confused.

I was counseling a new student who needed to talk about issues he was having at home with his parents. Imagine that! He was a nice kid, a big guy who was concerned about the safety of his much younger sister because of a violent dad. He came into our office once a week, and he and I spent an hour talking one-on-one in a private room. Initially, I expected that we would meet once or twice and that he would feel better and move on.

As it turned out, he was very unhappy and so concerned for his little sister's safety that he kept coming in to meet with me just to be able to talk and get whatever advice I could offer him. I could tell that I became a source of relief for him, and he looked forward to getting together each week. We met that entire semester. It felt good to be able to help him in any way I could. It also helped me with my own troubles. If nothing else, it opened my eyes to see that there were other people in my age group with problems as well. In that sense I was not alone.

I thought it took a lot of courage on his part to speak to a stranger, especially another student, about such serious and sensitive problems. I thought about my own problems at home and knew that I did not find it easy to speak to anyone about them. I was covering up my own issues, believing that I could overcome them all by myself by going to school, becoming educated, and working hard to improve my standard of living. That was not exactly accurate, however. None of that stuff gives you internal peace of mind. None of that cleanses your soul. At some point in your life, you have to find a way to let all the negativity out of you. Only then will you have inner calm.

My friends at Baruch came from middle-class families, for the most part. They lived in single-family homes or high-rise apartments. I was embarrassed that I lived with my parents in a small apartment under a subway station, with a broken window in my room, and infested with roaches and mice. I remember the day Cynthia stopped by to visit while she was home from Howard University. We were sitting on the bed talking, when suddenly she jumped up, startled by something. I turned to see what had jolted her. That's when I saw a cockroach walking on the wall.

She didn't say a word, but I could tell that she was embarrassed and disgusted. I was not about to share that environment with my college friends.

Some of my friends had cars and would invite me to their homes on weekends for parties or barbecues during the summer. I could never invite anyone to my home.

Richie Wieczerok was my closest friend at Baruch. He lived in Jamaica, Queens, with his parents in a nice middle-class home. They also had a summer home in Riverhead on Long Island, complete with a small motorboat. The boat was big enough for six people to sit in comfortably.

One weekend, Richie invited a bunch of us to his summer house for a barbecue and to go out on his boat. It was the first time I had ever been on a boat that size. We all had a great time speeding out on the Long Island Sound, except that I nearly fell out of the boat. I was standing in the front when Richie hit a wave. I flew up in the air and landed in the back as the boat sped forward. I didn't know how to swim, so I was glad I landed on the boat and not in the water—sans life preserver.

A few days later Richie told me that he was pissed at his parents because they scolded him for inviting another Baruch friend, Howard, because he was black. I was surprised—I didn't notice that anyone was uncomfortable when we were at the house. If they were upset, they hid it well. I didn't ask Richie, but I wondered if his parents were upset with him for inviting me as well because I was Puerto Rican. He never mentioned the story to Howard.

None of my friends at Baruch, including Richie, knew where I lived. I never wanted them to know that I was poor. Whenever we went out on weekends, I made excuses to meet Richie somewhere so he did not pick me up at my home.

One evening, Richie was going to pick up another friend near LaGuardia airport and insisted that he pick me up at my home so we could hang out. I tried to make some excuse to avoid having him come by, but it didn't make sense. When it came time to give him my address, I gave him my grandparents' address, which was at 31st Avenue and 94th Street, about five or six blocks from my home. My grandparents lived in a modest single-family home, a much nicer home than where we lived. I asked Richie to call me thirty minutes before he was going to arrive, on the pretext that I wanted to make sure I was ready.

When Richie called me, I told him I would be ready in thirty minutes. I walked down Junction Boulevard to my grandparents' house and waited outside on the front steps for Richie to arrive. I didn't ring the bell because I didn't want to go inside. I was hoping that no one would come out and see me just standing there. When Richie drove up, I pretended to be walking out by grabbing the door handle and then I walked down the stairs and into his car.

At the end of the night, I had him drop me off near a train station and I took the subway home. "No need to go out of your way to drop me off," I said. I remember feeling the stress of hiding where I lived because I was ashamed of the place. On the positive side, living in the cramped apartment gave me the motivation to strive for more. I wanted to make sure I could live in a larger home with plenty of space. It was a way for me to overcome the claustrophobic feeling I developed growing up in tight spaces with four siblings. It would take me years to achieve this goal, but I was determined to get there.

I thought that by elevating my standard of living and being responsible, I would certainly be different from my parents and break the cycle of negativity they taught me and my brothers and sisters. My life was a process of breaking out of the mold that my parents tried to naturally squeeze me into. I was destined not to fit in that frame.

As I developed relationships outside of my home, I continued to learn more about myself. I noticed that in my reaction to people, I was impatient and unforgiving. One evening at Jack in the Box, we were very busy attending to lots of customers. It was a Friday evening and one of the busiest days of the week for fast-food restaurants like ours. I was the shift manager and had a new female employee making tacos. I thought she was too slow in assembling them, so I yelled at her and commanded her to hurry up, in front of everyone, employees and customers (just like my parents used to do to me). The taco shells were fresh out of the fryer and too hot for her to handle.

I expected her to handle the hot shells carefully, but I did not communicate that to her. She was frightened and upset at how I yelled at her, and that did not help her to work any faster. I asked her to move aside and I made them myself. She quit the job at that instant and left.

Afterward I was ashamed at how I treated that employee. I did not teach her anything positive and I didn't coach her. Although I was only sixteen years old at the time, I was her leader and did a terrible job of mentoring her. That bothered me. I treated her the way my parents had treated me. I found myself reflecting on that each time I noticed myself behaving the way they behaved toward me. That realization encouraged me to work to be different. You can imagine how many thousands of times over many years I had to do this self-analysis and consciously adjust my own behavior. But I was determined to succeed in doing that.

Later that evening, a relative of the girl's came by the restaurant with a baseball bat to come after me. My friend Eddie, who was also working at the time, calmed him down and the guy left. Eddie later told me I needed to calm down and not talk to people the way I spoke to that girl. He was absolutely correct, and I learned from that experience that not everyone works at the same pace.

Another time, I had an argument with Cynthia in the lobby of my apartment building on Astoria Boulevard. The entry door had a small window in the center of the top half that was covered with wire mesh. I got angry at whatever we were arguing about and put my hand through the glass and wire. My hand was cut, but I didn't care. I was too angry to feel any pain. Cynthia and her family were calm people and my reaction frightened her, so she quickly went home. I was often angry and impatient with people. I found it difficult to accept mistakes. It did not matter if it was one made by someone else or by me. I reacted with uncontrolled anger either way.

This is the front door at the 94-04 Astoria Boulevard apartment where I put my fist through the screened window during an argument with Cynthia.

I learned over time that I was fighting the demons growing inside of me. My much maligned spirit was the product of years of punishment at the hands of my parents, and the violence and negativity that were standard protocol in our home. I believed I had to work extra hard to reverse the effects of the abusive behavior that was literally beaten into me over my growing years.

Perhaps the easy way out would have been to accept the violent nature I had developed rather than try to change, but I was driven almost my entire young life to be different, to follow a righteous path. I have never been comfortable doing something or following a path that I see as incomprehensible. Following in my parents' footsteps was simply out of character for me; it was unnatural. I had to do something different. I just needed enough time to figure out what that different something, that new path, was going to be for me. I had to be open to criticism by others in order to understand how people saw me, especially people I was close to who cared enough to bring to my attention that my reaction to the most minimal issue was usually a destructive overreaction.

This is how I learned to respond to mistakes: if I dropped a glass of milk, I got so angry with myself that I wasted my time fuming for far too long, stomping up and down, or punching a wall or table rather than expending energy to clean up the mess. There is no doubt in my mind that many of us spend an inordinate amount of time—hours, days, weeks, months, and sometimes years—standing still instead of moving forward. That is precisely what happened when I reacted with a fit of rage at the spilling of that glass of milk. I was so overcome with rage, I failed to see that I still had to clean up the mess. It was not going to clean itself up because I got angry.

If someone else did the same, I got just as angry and usually asked them, "How could you do that?" It would have been far easier and taken much less time and caused everyone, myself included, much less stress to simply clean up after the accident and move on. But that is what I learned at home: Seek blame and ridicule the culprit of the misdeed. It is all about punishment versus coaching. There are people who believe that punishing children, whether by spanking or a more severe form of physical response to misbehavior, will over the long term result in those children developing respect for others.

Is it respect for, or fear of, others?

In any case, fear also breeds mistrust, and that lack of trust in people was another challenge for me to overcome. Because of all the things I witnessed growing up, it was difficult for me to place trust in anyone. It was difficult for me to trust that my mom was looking out for my well-being. It was unfortunate that even Mom's working at a job resulted in negative outcomes.

It seemed that every job Mom managed to get when we needed money only lasted a few weeks. Deep down she had no desire to work. After a few weeks or so, her exit strategy haphazardly conceived, she began to complain at home about something that she didn't like at the job. Usually, it was a boss who was rude and condescending to her, or disrespectful of her as a female; or a coworker subjecting her to harassment. It became clear to me after a few of these occurrences that she simply did not want to work. I don't think she ever contemplated that with five kids and a husband who worked a factory job, the family would hit hard times and that she might have to go to work herself. Mom came from a family where her dad, my beloved grandfather Julio, was the lone breadwinner in their home, and they managed just fine, despite having a large family of eleven of fifteen surviving children. Grandma never had to go to work, and they survived without struggles, even buying their own home.

Having grown up in a time when the wife and mother stayed at home to care for the children and the home, while the man worked to provide financial support for the family, going to work was not something Mom expected to ever have to do. Nonetheless, when things got tight at home, she and Dad agreed that she had to get a job to help with the family expenses. So, from time to time Mom reluctantly went to work.

At one point she got a job doing security screening at LaGuardia airport. This was many years before the TSA and the current level of security. Back then in the seventies, anyone could walk to the gate area after walking through a metal detector, so the level of security staff was much lighter than today.

One afternoon she came home early from that job, complaining that she had to quit because she got into a fight with a male passenger and he threatened to harm her. I remember her telling us she couldn't go back there because she was afraid he was following her. Apparently, according to her, he was in the *mafia* and she was sure he was following her. I was only thirteen at the time and believed her. I was afraid for her, and for all of us, so I periodically peeked out the window through the drawn blinds to see if I saw men who looked like mobsters watching our apartment. I did that for two days. In retrospect, how could she have told us such a crazy story simply to justify quitting a job?

Once I extricated myself from my parents' hold, I thought I could stop the violence and negativity going forward and begin working on repairing myself. This was much easier said than done. I still needed a family, and I could not stop communicating with my parents entirely. My parents unintentionally tried to make it a bit easier with what I considered to be their final act of abandonment and my ultimate disappointment.

Chapter Twenty

One day as I was coming home from school, I reflected on the pleasant day. I was happy with my college courses, my new schoolmates, and all the programs I was involved in, including writing for the Baruch student newspaper, *The Ticker*. I got through my freshman year with good grades, and that gave me the confidence that I could succeed in college. Since I was the first one in my family among my siblings, parents, and even ten aunts and uncles to go to college, initially I questioned if I was smart enough to make it. But getting through that first year was important in establishing that I belonged at that level.

That afternoon I arrived at our apartment on Roosevelt Avenue in Corona and entered my room as usual. Mom walked in with Dad and informed me that the family was moving. Evelyn, the older of my two sisters, who was two years younger than me, was pregnant and going to live with her boyfriend, Percio. Nelson had already moved out and was living with his girlfriend and their new baby, Patricia, so named because she was born on St. Patrick's Day.

That meant that going to the new apartment—a ground-floor apartment in a modified single-family house on 31st Avenue and 94th Street in Jackson Heights, only a couple of blocks away from our original Queens apartment on Astoria Boulevard—would be my youngest sister and brother, Susan and Wil, and my parents and me. At least that is what I assumed. Mom, in a very nonchalant manner,

informed me that I could not move with them. I was
shocked by this news. "What do you mean?" I asked.

I remember feeling scared, not knowing what I would
do or where I would live. I could not understand why they
would abandon me. It did not occur to me that my parents
were disappointed in me for choosing to go to college and
improving my future prospects rather than working to
support them. In many respects, I was lucky that my nature
was to be a fighter and that I was determined to seek a
better future and not succumb to the status quo simply
because it is what they wanted. Still, being in that empty
apartment all alone gave a frightening finality to our
relationship.

If I had done as they wished, I would have remained in
Corona or Jackson Heights the rest of my life, working at
Jack in the Box. That would have pleased them, but not
me. My dad chimed in when Mom broke the news to me.
He informed me that there were still two weeks left on the
current month's rent, and even though they were leaving in
a few days, I was allowed to stay in the apartment until the
end of the month. I guess he felt that softened the blow by
giving me two weeks to find a new place to live.

He requested that when I left the apartment at the end
of the lease term, I return to them the twin bed I slept on,
the flimsy plywood dresser, and the aluminum double door
standing closet.

I remember feeling a sense of panic, wondering what I
was going to do. I thought it was entirely irresponsible of
them, and inconsiderate to disrupt my life during a critical
time of my development in school. But they didn't love me!
I had no idea how to look for a place to live, and my
parents offered no advice as to how I should begin.

I was also extremely sad and depressed that, while I
had felt for a long time that I did not have a family I could
depend on, or one that had a solid foundation built on

love, trust, coaching, and teaching, now I knew it was true, and the separation felt final.

It was September, and the weather was nice the day everyone moved out. The apartment was totally empty except for the refrigerator, the shower curtain, and the furniture in my room. I could smell the emptiness of the place as I walked through the apartment to see that they were indeed gone. I remember thinking that this may have been what my dad felt like the day he came home and saw that Mom had emptied the apartment and left him. I remember crying all by myself, with a heavy heart, at the confirmation that they didn't love me.

I was frightened at the prospect of sleeping there. A few months before, some guys broke into the jewelry and novelties store directly below our apartment, and all I could think about as I lay in bed was when the police came through our hallway with guns drawn, searching for the robbers. The thieves had broken in through a back window in a tight alleyway. Once the police got there, the thieves were blocked and apprehended quite easily.

I remember hearing noises that you can only hear when there is absolute silence in an empty place. Unable to sleep, I got dressed and went downstairs to hop on the Q33 bus, which stopped at Junction Boulevard and Roosevelt Avenue. I figured I might as well go to LaGuardia airport and spend the night in one of the open lounge areas. Having been there many times before, it was the most familiar place I could think of.

When I boarded the bus and walked to the back, I saw my dad sitting there. It was a little past midnight and he was on his way from work to his new home. I was surprised to see him and didn't feel like speaking to him. It was a strange feeling. He said hello and asked where I was going. I told him I was going to the airport. We did not speak any further until he simply said good-bye and got off the bus at the 32nd Avenue stop. It was a chilling encounter! The father/son relationship between us felt over. The fond memories—of going to Yankee games, just the two of us; him rescuing me from a bout of asthma by taking me to the emergency room at Lincoln Hospital in the Bronx when he found me wheezing in the living room late in the night; or showing off his son to coworkers when I accompanied him to his job at Sunshine Biscuits—were suddenly memories pushed to the back of that bus.

Was Dad disappointed in me because I chose not to follow in his footsteps? Was he disappointed because I chose instead to do better than he did? After all, sons have been continuing their fathers' businesses since at least the first century during Jesus's time: a carpenter like his father plying his trade. Was I then the ultimate disobedient son? If so, my wanting to be different was misunderstood. And usually a misunderstanding is a product of a lack of communication.

Seeing him only made me feel sadder than I already was, perhaps because it again confirmed that I was alone. I continued on my way to the airport, where I spent the night sitting in the lounge chairs and walking around. I couldn't sleep, but I wasn't afraid. I probably would have fallen asleep if I had not been in shock, distraught by the thought of being abandoned.

The next morning I returned to the apartment to shower and figure out what I was going to do, where I was going to live. I didn't want to stay in the apartment even though I had another two weeks on the lease.

I stopped by the laundromat on Junction Boulevard where I regularly washed my clothes. I wanted to review their message board in hopes of finding a cheap room to rent. I knew I could not afford an apartment, which might have cost $500 per month, so I was looking for a room to rent for much less. I did not imagine at that point in my life that I would ever need to move into a room. My vision was to finish college, get a good paying job in New York City, and rent an apartment in Manhattan. It was apparent that those plans would have to wait.

Ever since I delivered groceries in the city, my dream was to live in Manhattan. Of course, I had no idea how much apartments in the city cost, but it was part of what I aspired to do. Besides, it would get me away from Queens and my family. I didn't mind seeing them, especially my brothers and sisters (except for Nelson) and my aunts, uncles, and cousins, but I thought it was better to visit occasionally from a distance. It is like George Burns once said: "Happiness is having a large, loving, caring, close-knit family in another city."

I was lucky to find a room for rent in a single-family house in Corona. The woman who owned the house had modified it to rent out all the rooms on the second floor. She and her family lived on the first floor, which had a separate entrance. The upstairs tenants did not need to see the family downstairs in order to get to their rooms.

The room was a tiny space, probably eight feet by four feet, and had a low, slanted ceiling because of the roof line. The ceiling was probably six feet high at the highest point and five feet at the lowest. The woman asked for twenty-five dollars per week, and I immediately rented the room. I gave her the twenty-five dollars for the first week and arranged to move in the following Saturday.

The day I moved into the room, Nelson picked up the old furniture, the dresser, closet, and twin bed, to take to my parents as they requested. My new room had a twin bed and a small dresser, but the room was so small that I could not walk between the dresser and the bed. There was a window that looked out onto the street in front of the house. I had to share a bathroom and kitchen with the tenants of two other rooms on the second floor. I was disgusted to have to share the bathroom, and I never used the kitchen while living there. Other than that, the room and the house were pretty clean.

Sleeping there at night, I was filled with mixed feelings. On the one hand, I was depressed and still stunned that my parents had abandoned me. They didn't give me much warning. It wasn't like they said that once I finished college I would have to move out. On the other hand, it gave me more determination to succeed, and show them I could make a successful life for myself despite their lack of support and guidance.

It was in my nature to fight through challenges and not succumb to them. I believed I was born to be different. Maybe that is why my parents treated me so differently than my other siblings. They could not understand why I did not turn out to be like them.

From the time I was as young as five years old, I was looking for ways to make money. It gave me the independence to buy my own candy or spinning top, and I enjoyed that. I was born with a need to be independent. Maybe that is why I would always wake up so early in the morning and head outdoors. All the challenges I faced throughout my life were lessons for me to sharpen my focus and use as springboards to get to another level in my life.

Once I shook off the anger and sadness at my parents leaving me, I began to think about how I was going to get out of that room and into my first apartment. I was working part time at Siderius, helping them with data entry on their new IBM System 32 computer, and I knew they were looking for a full-time employee to assume the role of operator for the system. I told Steve Clayton that I could do the job and would change my schedule at Baruch the next semester and work full time for him. He liked the idea because I was a known entity. He knew I was dedicated to my work and he liked that. I also had the support of Joe

Cather, who assured Steve that I was a natural with the computer. They offered me the job, and I accepted the position for an annual salary of $13,000.

I was excited about my new job—my first full-time job in New York City. I felt the need to share the good news with someone, so I went to my parents' apartment to give them the news. A part of me felt it was natural to want to share with my parents and seek their good wishes. Another side wanted to show them that I was making progress in spite of them. I didn't expect them to be happy for me, but it made me feel good to show them that I was doing well.

Mom did not understand the concept of an annual salary. My dad worked as a laborer with an hourly wage, and that is all they understood. When I told her my new job paid $13,000 per year, she asked, "What does that mean?" She thought they were going to hand me that amount of money all at once. When I explained that I would get paid over the course of a year, she seemed confused and disappointed.

I was disappointed that I was not going back to Baruch full time for my junior year, but I was anxious to establish myself financially. I was tired of not having enough resources to support myself, and felt that was a bigger priority for me at the time. There were many aspects of life contributing to my impatience, but none more compelling than the lack of security and support at home.

At Siderius, I was expanding my responsibilities by working hard and volunteering to do more. I was always on the lookout for opportunities to pursue. When I generated the computer reports for managers, I noticed there were discrepancies in their inventory reports as compared to reports they were receiving from the leased warehouses at various ports throughout the country. The managers began to run into trouble with sales, and were accusing the Chinese of dumping steel onto the US market at much cheaper prices than their own. The slowdown in sales resulted in the company laying off some sales and administrative people.

It was a difficult time for the company, but an opportunity for me. My position was safe because I was the only person running the computer system. I suggested to the head of sales that I go to the warehouses and conduct a physical inventory to reconcile it with our computer records. The company had hired an industry consultant, Dick Timme, to help them with the reconciliation, and they sent me to the warehouses with him.

The first warehouse was in Chicago. Dick was a rough guy who got along well with the longshoremen working at the sites. Our job was to take a physical count of the rolls of steel, both in the yard and inside the warehouses. We had to identify those that had Siderius labels and document their attributes: type of steel, measurement in feet, and any other detail written on the visible sheet. In all, we visited warehouses in Chicago, San Diego, and Detroit. It was my very first business trip. I was nineteen years old and suddenly felt homesick, even though I lived alone in a small room. I had a girlfriend, Jeannette, who I met during my second year at Baruch. I remember calling her in the evening from my hotel room to complain about being homesick. I never called my parents. Jeannette had quickly become my new family.

I also didn't care much for Dick Timme. His personality was too rough for my liking. In Chicago, we stayed at a cheap motel. The best hotel we stayed at was the Pontchartrain in Detroit. It was a luxurious hotel with a long and rich history in the downtown area of the city.

Dick and I had dinner one evening at the rooftop restaurant of the Detroit Plaza Hotel, The Summit, which at the time was a brand-new hotel in downtown Detroit. I was thrilled because it had a revolving floor with large windows that entertained us with a 360-degree view of the city, the river, and Canada in the distance.

When Dick and I returned to New York, he reported our findings to the management team. We found that there were more Siderius rolls and sheets of steel in our physical inventory than was reported by some of the warehouses. Management was happy with this finding because they could sell more steel.

A couple of weeks later, I was asked if I could visit other warehouses and conduct physical inventories. I agreed, of course, and also told the manager I could do it by myself. I really didn't want to travel with Dick Timme again.

Management was happy not to have to pay him as a contractor if they could have me, an employee, do the work. So I went on the road, visiting a few more warehouses and finding additional inventory that was previously unreported by the warehouses. At the end of the project, I was awarded a bonus of $1,000.

In May of 1977, just one month shy of my twentieth birthday, I found out that Jeannette was pregnant. I was going to be a dad much earlier in life than I expected. I had mixed feelings about the news. On the one hand, I was thrilled that I was going to be a dad and have a family of my own. The thought of having a child I could nurture, hug, protect, educate, teach, and support was exciting to me. Yet I feared that having a child and being married at such a young age would inevitably interrupt my education and choke my freedom. Still, it was a chance to have a loving family life, and that was of paramount importance to me. In some ways it was an opportunity to prevail over the hardships of family life at home with my parents.

I was determined not to repeat the mistakes of my parents. I vowed that our child was going to be properly educated without worrying about money for tuition, food, or clothing. I also vowed that we would always live in a nice, clean home, where our child would be comfortable and proud to invite friends over to play.

Still I was terrified by the responsibility and how it might change my life. I didn't know if I was ready to commit my whole life to Jeannette either. It was one of the most stressful periods of my young life. But I was not going to shirk the responsibility of being a father, even though the prospect was overwhelming and all-consuming. I was also afraid of making the same mistakes that my parents made in raising the five of us.

There aren't any mandatory books or training classes to learn how to be a good parent. Maybe there is a basic flaw in nature that allows a person to physically conceive a child before being mentally prepared.

The reality was that neither Jeannette nor I had the wisdom to have a child. As I said before, I was nineteen, and she was seventeen. How could we know the magnitude of the responsibility of not only raising a child, but also managing a family? Obviously, we had no idea!

My number one priority was our child. I did not think of anything else. I knew that in order to prepare for the baby, who was going to be born in the winter, I had to get a new job with a higher salary. Although my major at Baruch was journalism, I was lucky to learn computer programming from Joe Cather while working at Siderius, and I had taken a couple of programming courses at school. That proved to be valuable for a lifetime.

Initially, I went for an interview as a staff writer at a magazine, but was quickly discouraged when I was told the annual salary was $15,000, which was about the same as I was making at Siderius. I was looking for much more than that. I began looking for computer programming jobs, and landed an interview with Standard Brands, a consumer foods corporation with headquarters at 460 Park Avenue,

right off 57th Street. It was a beautiful midtown loca-
tion. The company was the manufacturer of brands such as
Planters Nuts, Fleischmann's margarine, and many others.
It is now part of Nabisco.

After two or three interviews, I was offered a position
as a programmer to be part of the team that was working
on modifying and implementing the IBM MAPICS (Manu-
facturing, Accounting and Production Information Control
Systems) software for the various plants throughout the
country. We were based at headquarters and traveled
frequently to the various plants when the software was
ready for installation, and for training of the users. There
were two teams created, one for the Planters' division and
one for the Fleischmann's division.

I was offered a base salary of $23,000 to be part of the
Planters' development team; the primary locations we had
to visit were Suffolk, Virginia, and Fort Smith, Arkansas. It
was substantially more money than I was making at Siderius and I jumped at it. Months later, my project manager,
Mary Jane Range, confessed to me that they were willing to
offer me more, if I had requested it. I always remembered
that for future negotiations, but for the time being, I was
thrilled with the salary and the job.

I moved out of the one-room place I was renting by
the week, and Jeannette and I moved into a studio apartment in Flushing, Queens. The apartment was a big step up
for me, with its air-conditioning and elevator. The apartment in Flushing ushered in a transition for me in many
ways. I now had the responsibility of having rent to pay, a
refrigerator to fill, and a pregnant girlfriend.

My motivation for choosing to move to Flushing rather than Corona or nearby Jackson Heights was to be as
far away from family as I could afford. If I had the financial
means, I would have moved farther away, maybe to New
Jersey or Pennsylvania. I knew that someday I would seek

to move out of state, but for the time being, I happily settled for the apartment in Flushing.

Once I was on my own, I still feared that I would turn out to be just like my parents. Even though I knew deep inside that I wanted to be different, I constantly worried that I would become a product of my past environment. My behavior in everything I did was inevitably based on a combination of the way my parents taught me and my innate attributes as a person. These two traits always seemed to be in conflict with each other. I firmly believed that my nature was more powerful than the lessons from my past, which propelled me to ultimately take the right path in my life.

There were many times I could have succumbed to my background and become just like my parents, or worse. I could have followed some of my friends and become a drug addict, a dropout, or remained a gang member. I could have ended up in jail or, worse, dead. I saw my best friend Cheo Martinez wind up in and out of Riker's Island. His sister, Carmen, who married and divorced Ivan, died of AIDS, caused by an ex-con drug addict she dated after she and Ivan divorced. Other friends did time in prison for murder.

A year after we moved to Queens, I went to the South Bronx by train to visit friends. I was stunned to see Jose, the kid who lived next door to us on Vyse Avenue and whose dad shot himself, leaning against a building stoned out of his mind. I could not believe he had gotten into drugs at the age of thirteen. I didn't speak to him out of fear. Years later I wondered what ever happened to him. Did he die of a heroin overdose?

I wanted to be a person who could be trusted and, most importantly, to be trusting of others. I spent a great deal of time as an adult looking in the mirror, literally and figuratively, in order to self-assess and improve my behavior.

No one knew, but each time I got angry, I asked myself if I reacted in such a way because it was what my parents would do. That is how I taught myself how to control my temper. It was also important for me to work hard to become self-sufficient. I did not want to depend on anyone for my livelihood the way my parents did. I wanted to control my own destiny. And I wanted to make sure that my daughter was loved and cared for so she could grow up a happy child.

Whenever I am driving in my car and the satellite radio plays "Cat's in the Cradle" by Harry Chapin, I have heavy mixed emotions. I think it is a great song that symbolizes the inevitability of a child growing up to be just like his dad. When the child is young and wants to emulate his dad, his father does not pay attention to him when he says, "I'm gonna be like you, Dad. You know I'm gonna be like you." The child wants his dad to play with him, but the father does not have the time. When the dad is retired and wants to visit with his son, the son does not have time. The dad says, "And as I hung up the phone it occurred to me, he'd grown up just like me, my boy was just like me." I cry every time I hear that song. It saddens me that I never wanted to be like my father.

Chapter Twenty-One

November 26, 1977.

That is a date that changed my life forever! Jeannette was staying at her mother's and was in her seventh month of pregnancy. At 5 a.m. that 330th day of the year, on a cold Saturday, I got a call from Jeannette's mom. Jeannette had given birth prematurely to a baby girl. I hurriedly got dressed and rushed to Elmhurst General Hospital. The Main Street, Flushing train was some five long blocks away from our apartment, and the best way I could think of to get to the train station was to run the entire way. I could not wait around for a bus or a taxi. It was early morning and the streets were still quiet; after all, it was a Saturday.

I got to the train station, huffing and puffing from my run. The Main Street station of the Flushing Line is the start (or end, depending on whether you are coming or going) of that line, so there is usually a train there waiting for its departure time. I boarded the train and anxiously waited for the doors to close. It seemed like an eternity! It was like watching water boiling. Finally, the doors closed and the train left the station.

When we arrived at the 82nd Street Station, I ran as fast as I could down the stairs and the few blocks to the hospital. Somehow, I made it to the maternity ward and to Jeannette's room. The first thing I wanted to know was how the baby was. I wanted to see her. Suddenly, I didn't feel alone. The solitary confinement that had been prevalent for years in my life was instantly abolished with the seemingly simple event of the birth of my beautiful daughter. We named her Janie. After seeing Jeannette, I walked over to the nursery to find baby Janie's incubator. She was beautiful! It felt absolutely phenomenal to see a living, breathing human being who I helped to create.

Again, and in retrospect, Jeannette and I were both too young in years and preparation to comprehend the magnitude of what lay before us. The future was going to be a work in progress. We were going to learn how to raise a child in real time, without the benefit of proper coaching and preparation in our own upbringing.

Jeannette's family background was not so different from my own, and perhaps worse in some aspects. Her parents were divorced, her father a rough and physically violent man, and her brother was a troubled and mentally unstable young man. Perhaps I should have known that it wasn't the best choice of a family to be a part of, but I was blinded by my deep inner need for a family. And, while my parents rejected me, Jeannette's mother embraced me. Stella was a good woman caught up in a bad, violent marriage herself. She was a hardworking woman who seemed to have no problem being the chief breadwinner for her family. The two older sisters lived nearby—one was married and the other a single mom of three.

I failed to make a connection between the son's mental problems and the father's personality. Several times I accompanied Jeannette and Stella to mental institutions where Ezekiel had been admitted. Once, we went to see him in the mental ward of Elmhurst Hospital, but we were not allowed to see him because he was being restrained in a solitary room. I did not know why he had been brought there, but it didn't matter to me. It seemed we were all safer with him behind a secured door.

Eventually, Ezekiel was admitted for a long stretch (months) at a Long Island institution for mentally disabled people. I accompanied Jeannette and Stella there for a visit with Ezekiel during the summer of 1976. We sat on a bench on the grounds while we waited for him to be brought out. It eerily reminded me of a scene in a movie where sedated patients walk the grounds to get some recreational walking and breathe fresh air, under the watchful eye of medical staff in close proximity. Ezekiel came out and seemed happy, smiling and joking as he sat and walked with us. The strange thing is that if not for his frequent uncontrollable outbursts, he appeared rather normal. But he was not! He was a very troubled young man.

This was the family I was destined to join in order to bring a child into the world and thereby create the family life I craved. I very much looked forward to hugging, feeding, changing, and kissing that beautiful baby. I had visions of teaching her to swim or, more realistically, providing her with swimming lessons; helping her with homework projects; teaching her to ride a tricycle, then a bicycle; watching her grow and speak her first words, take her first steps. One day she would graduate from kindergarten, junior high school, high school, and college. And I would be there for each and every occasion! Part of my mission, and responsibility, as a parent would be to ensure that Janie had the parental love that is characteristic of a self-confident person.

Because Janie was born a preemie (at seven months) and weighed less than four pounds, she had to remain in the hospital until her weight increased to five pounds. That was our first challenge as parents, and first disappointment—not being able to take our baby home when Mom left the hospital. We both felt awkward and scared. How could it be that we could not take our child home? How could the hospital tell us that? After all, she was our child! Our natural instinct was to protect our child and we could not do that. That scared us! Her well-being was in the hands of the hospital staff.

Just a day went by when we got a call from the hospital that we needed to go see Janie, that she had jaundice. *What in the world is that? Is she going to make it? Are we going to lose her?* What would we do if we lost the baby? I was still trying to get over the fact that when I first saw my daughter in the nursery, her legs were folded over to her torso. I immediately asked the nurse what was wrong with her legs and was told that she was born breech and that her legs would come down soon. *Breech? What the hell is that? She can't walk like that!* I was assured that she would be fine in a few days. Now the jaundice! We were told that this was normal for a preemie baby and she would be fine. She was eating, or drinking formula, well, and her weight was slowly increasing as she lay in the incubator with heat lamps above her.

Still, I was apprehensive about the jaundiced yellowing of her skin. It might have been more helpful to tell us the specific medical causes of this condition rather than saying it was normal and would go away. Being a detailed thinker, I would have felt more at ease if the nurses had told us that jaundice is caused by an excess amount of bilirubin, which causes the yellow coloring and is a normal part of the pigment released from the breakdown of used red blood cells. It is normally filtered by the liver and released into the intestinal tract. A newborn's liver, especially a premature one, often can't remove the bilirubin quickly enough, causing an excess of bilirubin and thus the yellowing of the skin. As the liver matures, the condition disappears. I might have rested easier with that knowledge.

Only two days and I felt as though we had already had to deal with a whirlwind of challenges. I could not even imagine what the next months, years, decades were going to be like. What was certain was that just like the first two days, from now on my life was destined to be all about Janie.

Each day we visited Janie at the hospital, anxiously checking on her weight in hopes of being able to take her home with us. Each of the first few days, we were disappointed! Finally, on the fifth day we were told that she had reached five pounds and she could go home. I had never in my young life felt the exhilaration that I felt upon becoming a father. It was as if I had received the greatest gift one can receive. Despite her being born a preemie, underweight, breech, and jaundiced, she was healthy and beautiful!

Of course, neither Jeannette nor I knew what to expect once we brought Janie home. It was a brand-new experience with a mountain of responsibility. The first few nights at home turned out to be largely sleepless ones. We placed the baby's crib near our bed so we could respond to her as necessary. With every whimper and every movement the baby made, I jumped out of bed to check on her. I wanted to make sure she was okay and not suffocating underneath her blanket. I was adapting to my incredibly changed life.

Going back to work was difficult, but it had to be done. After all, now more than ever, I had to provide for the family. I was preoccupied with thoughts of all the things I wanted to offer Janie in her infant life: food, good winter clothes, toys, and dolls, whatever I saw in stores for a baby her age.

As time passed, Janie grew and learned to smile and recognize us as her parents. It seemed that every day of her development, she rewarded us with a new reason to smile: her first tooth; her surprised look at seeing and then biting into a cob of corn; her first steps; the smile on her face each time she saw me come home from work. For first-time parents these experiences and more were endless nibbles of pure pleasure. It was an amazing feeling to love this tiny human being. Suddenly, I was no longer entangled in the web that was my hurtful family relationship with my own parents. That is how powerful the love of a child can be—the positive energy I felt. It was confusing because Mom and Dad must have felt the same exhilaration when I was born, but something changed dramatically over the years. I didn't understand then how that could happen.

When Janie was three years old, I switched jobs and went from Standard Brands to Cushman and Wakefield, Inc., a commercial real estate business located on Avenue of the Americas and 45th Street at the time. The new job paid considerably more money, so we were able to move into a larger apartment in the same building in Flushing. I also did not have to travel as I had to at Standard Brands, and that allowed me to spend more time with Janie, which I thoroughly enjoyed.

My relationship with Jeannette, however, was not going as well. We were very different people and were not getting along. The unfortunate fact was that while I loved being a father to Janie, I questioned my love for Jeannette. As we drifted apart, it was only inevitable that our marriage would slowly dissolve. Our relationship could not survive the many emotional vicissitudes that dominated our everyday lives. I could not help but remember the marital troubles Mom and Dad faced and how I vowed, upon witnessing their trials and tribulations, never to remain in an unhealthy relationship. I was quite stubborn on that point.

As the breakup seemed more and more imminent, I turned to ponder what I would do without being in Janie's life on a daily basis. It was always my dream to be the involved father that I did not have when growing up. That meant checking her homework when she started school; taking her to swimming lessons; teaching her to ride a bike;

taking her shopping for clothes; watching her play in the park; and guiding her to be a self-confident young lady. Now all of that was in jeopardy. My dream was vanishing and that depressed me.

Finally, after much discussion and many heated arguments with Jeannette, I moved out of the apartment and rented a studio apartment about a mile away. I figured that by staying close, I could easily be there for Janie as often as possible. I could still be a close father to her. My apartment was on the second floor of a four- or five-story building. It faced the front of the building and had a nice terrace. The morning after I moved in, I woke up and opened the terrace door. It was during the summer of 1981, and it was a bright, sunny morning. I walked out onto the terrace and stretched my arms to relax the tightness in my muscles. I took a deep breath, inhaling deeply as I felt my lungs expand. When I exhaled I felt a sense of liberation. I was free from a relationship that I did not want to be in any longer.

But I missed Janie terribly. She was an innocent human being and I had let her down, though she did not know it or could not comprehend it yet. I soon realized that I did not want to help raise Janie from a distance. Over the next couple of months, Jeannette and I talked about getting back together. In contemplation after our talks, I concluded that my motivation for considering reconciliation was my burning desire to fulfill my responsibility to my child. Reconciliation was not the right answer, and I knew it.

I had to do something else. I got into my car and sped to Jeannette's apartment, but there was no one home. I felt a sense of panic. Maybe she had moved away so that I couldn't see Janie. My reaction was to drive to her mother's house, hoping to find her and Janie there. As I sped out of the entrance to the building, a small poodle ran out of the front door of the apartment building across the street, directly under my car. I stopped immediately and got out. The poor puppy was not well. Its owner was heartbroken. He held the puppy in his arms and we drove to a veterinarian on Northern Boulevard a short distance away. Unfortunately, the puppy did not make it. I apologized to his owner and tried to console him. He was distraught, but acknowledged that the puppy ran out and he should have had him leashed. Still, I felt terrible!

I drove him back to the apartment building, where I saw Jeannette and Janie arriving home. I broke the news to Jeannette that it was not possible for us to get back together as husband and wife. What I said next I expected to be received with astonishment and rejection. I imagined that it was only natural for a mother to respond as I expected, and I prepared for a combative conversation.

I told Jeannette that although we could not get back together, I wanted Janie to live with me. "If we can't get back together, then I will join the Army and Janie can live with you," was her utterly surprising response. I was pleased how easy it was to be responsible for raising Janie, and simultaneously perplexed that Jeannette, a mother, could so easily give up her daughter. It was a decision I will never understand, no matter how many ways I try to rationalize it.

But that is what happened. Janie came to live with me in the studio terrace apartment, and Jeannette enlisted in the Army. I had become a twenty-three-year-old single father. To formalize my monumental responsibility, which I was too lacking in experience and wisdom to actually comprehend, I called my old neighborhood friend, Carlos Ferreira. He had since graduated from Kansas State University and passed the bar exam in New York State, and was practicing law. Carlos drew up the divorce papers, which stipulated that I was to have full custody of Janie.

Jeannette signed the papers, and just that simply I was a single father.

Most people, upon hearing that I was a single father at the age of twenty-three, invariably comment how difficult it must have been to raise a child, especially a little girl, as a single dad. But because I saw it as my responsibility and had faith that I was doing the right thing, I never stopped to wonder how difficult it might have been. I suppose if I had done that, I might have frightened myself out of going down that path. But it was what I wanted to do, and I was committed to give it my full attention.

The next twenty years, as Janie grew into a young lady, were filled with many challenges and adjustments. But every night that I tucked her in and kissed her good night, I thanked God for having such a beautiful girl and being able to raise her and give her a future that she could be happy with and proud of. I welcomed with open arms and anticipation the next chapter of my life as a single dad.

My beautiful Janie as she walked toward daddy near our Flushing apartment. She was two years old.

The supermarket on Astoria Boulevard and 99th -100 Streets where I bagged groceries for extra cash on Saturdays. The neighborhood has changed, as has the name of the supermarket.

The sweet joy as baby Janie and Dad hugged, sitting on a swing at a park in Flushing - 1979.

My grandparents' home in Jackson Heights.

Epilogue

I have often heard that every one of us has a destiny, that from the day you are born, if not from the moment of your very creation, God has determined your ultimate end. To continue that thinking, it is said that he then works backward from where he determines you will end up to draw the map that your life's journey will travel. It is this predetermined destiny that inspires many people to proclaim that "everything happens for a reason."

There are some people who fully embrace this belief and others who consider it a defeatist way of thinking. I am one of those who believe that things happen for a reason, although I also subscribe to the philosophy that you can determine your own destiny, or at least alter your journey in life. Life is a series of actions and reactions, after all.

There are plenty of examples throughout history of David and Goliath stories where the underdog or disadvantaged refused to accept the circumstances handed to them and persevered to ultimately triumph. A number of these can be found in Malcolm Gladwell's excellent book, *David and Goliath: Underdogs, Misfits, and the Art of Battling Giants.*

Gladwell shares the story of one Gary Cohn, who most people, including his mother, did not expect to amount to much of anything when he was a kid because he was dyslexic. In *David and Goliath*, Cohn is quoted recalling part of his childhood in school: "You know what it's like, you're a six- or seven- or eight-year-old kid, and you're in a public school setting, and everyone thinks you're an idiot, so you try to do funny things to try to create some social esteem." A couple of paragraphs later Gladwell adds, referring to Cohn's decision to try to talk his way into a job on Wall Street:

"He was selling aluminum siding. His mother thought that he would be lucky to end up a truck driver. He had been kicked out of schools and dismissed as an idiot, and even as an adult, it took him six hours to read twenty-two pages because he had to work his way word by word to make sure he understood what he was reading. He had nothing to lose."

And Cohn adds, "My upbringing allowed me to be comfortable with failure. The one trait in a lot of dyslexic people I know is that by the time we got out of college, our ability to deal with failure was very highly developed. And so we look at most situations and see much more of the upside than the downside. Because we're so accustomed to the downside. It doesn't faze us. I've thought about it many times, I really have, because it defined who I am. I wouldn't be where I am today without my dyslexia. I never would have taken that first chance."

And the point of this underdog story is that Gary Cohn went on to triumph over his dyslexia to become the president of Goldman Sachs.

In many ways I am grateful to my parents. I don't know if the way I was brought up was preordained, but it was what I had to deal with. And the first gift my parents gave me was my name—Israel. It was, and is, a name of significance, whether by coincidence or part of the great plan for my life.

In Genesis 35:10, after Jacob struggles with God and perseveres to be triumphant, God changes his name to Israel. The name, depending on the context, can mean "he who prevails with God." My own struggles with my belief in God, long in years and exhausting, eventually reached a resolution and my faith was restored. I concluded that God was not punishing me. He was preparing me for my life's triumphs by laying before me challenges to test my spirit of determination and guide me in building my courage.

I would not be where I am today if I had not gone through all of the challenges I endured growing up. And for that I am grateful to my parents.

Anyone who is faced with a disadvantage or a handicap or sees themselves as an underdog can overcome it and use it as a springboard to conquer the ordeal and find success in life. Listen to your innermost voice, to your gut, and when you hear that voice tell you, "I don't want to be here. I want to be up there," you will find the courage to follow the right path!